I'm Okay, If You're Okay

ENDORSEMENTS

"PTSD is an invisible battle that far too many veterans, first responders, and families fight in silence. *I'm Okay, If You're Okay* is a powerful and deeply human reminder that even the strongest among us can carry wounds no one else can see. Chris AuCoin's story is heartbreaking, courageous, and incredibly important. My hope is that this book helps spark more conversations, greater compassion, and real support for those struggling with trauma, addiction, and mental health challenges. At Paws of War, we see every day how healing, connection, and purpose can save lives, and this book shines a much-needed light on that mission."

— **Robert Misseri**, Co-Founder, Paws of War

"As someone who has lived in the worlds of combat, trauma, leadership, and service, *I'm Okay, If You're Okay* hit me hard. Chris AuCoin's story is not just about a Marine, a police officer, or a SWAT Commander, it's about a man who carried the weight of responsibility, pain, and expectation until it became unbearable. This book courageously exposes the silent war so many veterans, first responders, and families are fighting behind closed doors. It's raw, heartbreaking, deeply human, and desperately needed. More than a memoir of loss, it's a warning, a resource, and a call to action for anyone who believes strength means suffering in silence. Chris's story matters-and this book may very well save lives"

— **Remi Adeleke**, former U.S. Navy SEAL and bestselling author of *Transformed*

I'M OKAY, IF YOU'RE OKAY

THE CHRIS AUCOIN STORY

JENNIFER VAUGHN

HIP

Published by Huntsville Independent Press

2112 Morningside Drive NW, Huntsville, AL, 35810

I'm Okay If You're Okay is a true story, told as creative nonfiction, it reflects the author's account of real people and real events, set down at the family's request with nothing changed.

Major Chris AuCoin: your watch is over, and your story will stand. Rest easy.

Huntsville Independent Press can bring authors to your live event. For more information or to book an event, contact Huntsville Independent Press at +1 (256) 678-0411 or visit our website at www.HuntsvilleIndependent.com.

Cover design by Chris Treccani - 3 Dog Creative
Interior design by Chris Treccani - 3 Dog Creative

The text for this book was set in Adobe Garamond Pro.

Manufactured in the United States of America
First HIP paperback edition July 2026

12345678910

The Library of Congress has cataloged the hardcover edition as follows:

Names: Jennifer Vaughn, author.

Title: I'm Okay If You're Okay

LCCN (Pending)
Identifiers: ISBN 979-8-9957830-4-6 (pbk)
ISBN 979-8-9957830-5-3 (hcv)
ISBN 979-8-9957830-6-0 (ebook)

This book is dedicated to the men and women who stand to serve this nation without fear or hestitation. They are first in line to go, and often the last to come home, patrolling our streets, keeping our communities and country protected from those who would dare harm the innocent. They exhibit a certainty of mission, and a selfless desire to sacrifice—at times, operating in the shadows, where unspeakable danger lurks and evil threatens our way of life. They quietly guard the perimeters, protecting the fragile line between life and loss, at times handing over parts of themselves in the process. We must ask ourselves, have we done enough to support them in return, and if not, why? As you read this book, make a promise to yourself and every family who grieves a warrior lost to invisible wounds, to remove the flawed code of silence. Be their voice. Speak of them. Remember their duty, purpose, and memories, for they are all ours to carry now.

CONTENTS

FOREWORD

I have a confession to make. I have been known to skip a foreword when I read a book. I am not impatient by nature, but when I read, I am eager to get to the "real read" as fast as I can. It is ironic, perhaps, that I now have the privilege of writing the foreword to this powerful book, and I want to urge you to slow down. Take a breath. Allow me to ease you into this experience. What if reading a foreword gives the reader a taste, like an appetizer before dinner, of what's to come? What if it gets the reader ready for the story ahead, like an orientation for what lies ahead because the journey is sure to be a rough, yet important one? That is the foreword that I want to write here for *I'm Okay If You're Okay*, author Jennifer Vaughn's linear narrative into veteran and first responder Chris AuCoin's life. And to his death. She paints AuCoin in a rich palette that is sometimes glaring, and often stained red, but can never be mistaken as black and white. She generously and patiently allows us to walk and talk, cry, and even scream along with his family and friends who worked so hard to rid Chris of his demons. Along the way, you will read how the well-informed and well-intended, but ultimately unsuccessful, mental health system that might have helped was unable to save him.

Chris's story and the accompanying journey that he, his family, colleagues, and beloved friends traveled is not an easy one to read, sometimes requiring us to tap into our wisdom to navigate such a tortuous path. If you or your loved ones already know this path, beware that Chris's story can be triggering. You may need to press pause for a time, putting the book down for a break to digest. Do go one step at a time to keep both of your feet solidly on the ground. Give yourself that permission, so that when you finally reach the last page, three things are true: you have a better understanding of the complications of mental health and addiction, you remember to celebrate an American hero's life, *and* you have practiced self-care along the way.

Why should you take this journey? Because it is a true story of one person's life, and because Chris AuCoin is every one of us. An ordinary man who both embraced and endured extraordinary events with the best of intentions. He is as much a hero as he is a victim. Vaughn's compassionate and empathic view of Chris's odyssey is at once a biography, cultural anthropology essay as it is psychological theory. It is a look into our mental health systems, an essay on shame and stigma associated with cumulative PTSD and addiction, an expose on the failures of well-intentioned addiction programs, a white paper documenting how our military and first responder cultures address mental health, and a celebration of how loving family, colleagues, and friends can go beyond what seems humanly possible to rescue loved ones and end up nonetheless profoundly grieving the loss of their lives.

I'm Okay If You're Okay will leave you weeping and raging at the inequities of life, as well as embracing the incredible power of love all at once. It will scare you and defeat you and then build you back stronger than you were when you started at Chapter One. Why would you read this story if it might be so painful? My question is, why wouldn't you? We have a responsibility to Chris and to all those whom we love to be prepared for pain, to learn how to overcome hopelessness, to accept that no one can walk this path alone, and to better understand the resources that should be there but are not always available, or even accessible. Even if you do not read this story for yourself, read it because it may help you change another person's story, maybe even rewrite an ending that otherwise might have been tragic.

I have been a practicing clinical psychologist for over forty years. Thousands of men, women, teens, and children have generously allowed me to briefly accompany them on their journeys of hopelessness, despair, pain, and life questions. As a mental health professional, daughter, wife, mother, and now grandmother, I often ask myself how far would I go to save a loved one. Chris's journey, so eloquently captured here, will likely prompt you to ask yourself the same question. I will tell you now that there are no rule books. No prescribed nor absolute correct answers. But, there is love and hope and a multitude of practical resources that you can muster up and rely on along the way. Love and hope and resources are what Chris's parents, friends, and colleagues had to offer him, over and over again, for a decade. This story is as much about how these survivors cared for themselves as it is the story of their herculean efforts to care for their beloved son, brother, husband, father, friend, and colleague. You know the end of this story, you already know that Chris did not survive his journey. Perhaps you can imagine the pain of his death and what it might mean to his loved ones. And how despite the fluctuations of that pain, it will never truly end in their hearts. What we can't know but we must learn, is what Vaughn helps us to navigate as we go forward from here.

Finally, this book is about finding the last embers of hope, and using them to rekindle life. It is about how we can all join together to end the tragic path that leads some to suicide. I like to think that with all of the resources that are out there and with a lot of hard, even painful, work, we can do better. I do believe that Chris' death and the path that he walked leading up to it does *not* have to be your story. It does *not* have to be the ending of too many stories that have been told up until today. Today, there were 22 plus deaths by suicide amongst veterans and first responders in the United States. There were 22 others yesterday and there will likely be 22 more tomorrow. Yet we, *together*, can change that. Chris' story can help to show us how. I am an ever-hopeful soul who also knows that there are thousands of individuals who get help and survive, going on to live beautiful, precious lives. I am also here to tell you that there are literally thousands of professionals and peer counselors available right now to provide you help and support! I know that, like Chris' family, friends, and colleagues, there are countless compassionate and generous people who will go the distance and be a safe haven for you and your loved ones.

Chris's legacy is not in the way his life ended. It is in his life of service for his country. It is reflected in the profound love that he had for his family, colleagues, and friends. And while it is not the legacy that he had planned for when he started out in life, it is now one that hopefully will raise awareness, educate, and prevent suicide.

One last note in this foreword, but perhaps the most important: If at any point while reading you feel overwhelmed or triggered by the intensity of this story, please give yourself permission to take a break. If you feel, in any way, at risk for self harm or worried about a loved one, neighbor, colleague, or friend, please skip to the end of the book to the Resource Guide chapter for assistance. And most important of all, if you or someone you know is at imminent risk for self harm or suicide, please call 911, 988, or go to your local emergency room.

Thank you for pausing to read this foreword. Thank you for celebrating Chris AuCoin's life, and thank you for keeping yourself and the people whom you love safe.

—Dr. Laura Landerman-Garber
Hollis, New Hampshire
2026

CHAPTER 1

DECEMBER 7TH, 2022. THE DARKEST NIGHT

On a clear night, sundown in New Hampshire rolled across the land much like the slow opening of a treasure chest. Nestled within the expanse of sky, a bounty of gemstones came out to play, twinkling so bright you could almost pinch your fingers around one and bring it home as a souvenir. On a good night, nighttime in New Hampshire was nothing short of magical.

That early December evening, not a single star held enough shine to break through a blackness that was deeper than dark. A soulless void that hung over the earth with the sort of ferocious foreboding you could feel in your gut. A raw and dour Wednesday, icy rain fell on winter-frozen husks of matted grass and muck, releasing a pungent aroma of blight and nature's plunge into seasonal decay.

Brent AuCoin's throat was getting raw, strained by the cold and hours of calling out the name of his oldest son, but receiving no reply.

Chris!

Chris!

Just tell us where you are, Chris. We're coming.

We're coming!

Brent and his youngest son, Chad, were tracking Chris on their phones. His location dot revealed they were close. They'd followed Chris's location to the woods across the street from his house, where a dirt road led them to towering power lines. Even though technology told them Chris was near, he was not responding to their hollers and pleas extending into the frosty smog of heavy breathing and heartache.

Their watery eyes squinted into the square illumination of their phones as the dot pinged and shifted away. Chris was close but, on the move, yet again.

Chris!

Chris, please answer. We're coming!

They were up against a master. A former marine who had trained his body and mind to adapt to any hindrance—to conquer and survive. He was one with the cold, equal with the rugged landscape, inferior to nothing. Yet survival on this darkest night may not have been the mission. It stuck in their throats—that tremendous fear of what Chris had become—and the hours ticked by.

Chris!

Paula AuCoin was miles away, yet her heart was right there in those woods. She decided she would wait at home for word from Brent and Chad. Chris had done this before, so many times, and he'd always returned from the ragged edge, having ridden out the anguish alone—temporarily unlocked from the solitary battle with the demons who had grown so strong in ten years' time. Like an intermission in the tussle, the demons retreated, Chris earned a reprieve, and his family released itself from a ceaseless stance of impending doom. But that heaviness never really went away. If she'd learned anything in the last decade, it was this: Demons were patient, ever present, and could sniff out the slightest crack in her son's resolve.

Paula replayed a phone call she'd had with Chris hours earlier in her head, analyzing his tone and precise wording. He was upset, sobbing even, as he often did now, but this time it centered around her. A rapid and intense discussion that erupted during another explosive episode had relayed misinformation to Chris. He felt a betrayal and assigned blame Paula knew wasn't hers, yet she bore it fully that night for her son. The pain was unbearable and whole, as though a chasm had opened beneath her and was pulling her into an inescapable abyss as dark as the night outside her window. Chris had asked her for something during that call.

"Release me, Mom," he'd cried. "You always make me feel so guilty. Please, please, release me."

Paula's intellectual reasoning pinged on a level that put that request into an unspeakable category of despair. An existential quandary she couldn't shake. She'd tried to hold Chris right there with her. She had to keep him talking.

"Chris, wait. Wait! Everything I've ever done was to help you. Please understand, I love you, Chris. I have only ever loved you."

Chris moaned. His voice caught in another warbling cry. He continued to beg her.

"Mom, listen. Please listen. Release me, Mom. Please, release me."

Eventually, as she always tried to do with her oldest son, Paula gave him what he needed in that moment. In her heart, she knew the pain Chris was in. The suffering he'd endured. It had been so long. Too long.

"Okay, okay, Chris. Okay. I release you, Chris."

What else could she have said? Her son was in a catastrophic spiral, and she would've handed over her own life if he'd asked her to. Yet, even as she'd spoken the words, Paula felt a cascade of sorrow. Exactly what did that declaration mean and why did her son need it from her now?

Chris!

—★—

1:00 A.M.

Phone batteries were dimming, gloved fingers numbing, and a wicked wind blew against Brent and Chad's reddened skin. Chris's location dot was still visible, but he was still not responding to their shouts and pleas. They traversed around spiky, twisted apple trees whose fruit was long since plucked away and peered behind craggy rocks and ridged rises along the lumpy potholed land. Tree limbs weighed down by heavy rain acted like a protective blanket, tucking away whatever—and whomever—crouched beneath them. Chris knew how to fade into his surroundings, escape into the overcast, and wait out his pursuers. He had entered those woods behind his house the day before prepared to remain in them for a while. To battle the demons who'd emerged from the shadows of his mind yet again, on his own turf, and in his own way.

Brent had a choice to make. They were maneuvering farther down the power lines. Chad had little kids he needed to get home to. While Brent would have searched all night long in the dangerous cold, Chad had a family waiting on him—and that was an enormous responsibility he felt deeply.

Chris!

2:00 A.M.

Chris's phone must've died. He wasn't responding yet his dot was static. Bitter cold broke through weatherproof layers and Brent shivered. Exhausted, yet determined, he walked on. Screaming for his son.

No response ever came.

He watched Chad, knowing his unspoken alarm and cold fear of what his brother was capable of when cornered. Chad's wife and children tucked into their homes, waiting for their husband and father to return. Brent's choices were limited and burdensome. He took the chilled air into his lungs, held it there, and released it. His decision to leave relied on the favored history of their last miserable decade filled by close calls and near misses that Chris had survived. Brent halted his stride through the thorns and underbrush that clung like staples to his pant legs. He told himself Chris was safe out there in his element. Prepared and protected. As he'd been before. They'd always been able to get to him in time. To pull Chris back. This was just another bad night like all the rest. Chad was a father himself. He needed to be with his own family. While Brent would've searched for Chris forever, he had to make sure Chad got home that night.

He also knew Paula was back at their house, awake and worried about them out there in the freezing woods. He owed it to her, too, to return home. As a family, they had learned to make crisis decisions based on potential outcomes. If they called in reinforcements, and police arrived with guns drawn, Chris had already warned them of the confrontation that would force. Sure, they'd find him, likely easily, but Chris—and his family—were aware of exactly what that might yield.

No, Brent would not call the police, some who'd worked alongside Chris for years, relying on his calm guidance and experienced expertise in the most stressful, grueling moments their job had delivered. Paula would not call the police. Chris's wife, Tracy, and all three of his daughters would not call the police, nor would his two brothers. They would, as a family, make the impossible decision yet again to leave Chris in the woods behind his home, while they tried to wrestle their frantic minds from the brink of collapse.

They'd try to coax him out again when daylight broke along the horizon.

2:30 A.M.

Brent and Chad turned back and followed the power lines to the dirt road where they'd left their cars. It physically hurt them both—like a sucker punch to the ribs—to see Chris's house, knowing he wasn't inside with his family. Before they drove off, Brent and Chad shared a prayer, one of millions that had come before, that Chris would be watched over and protected until they found him again, safe and sound.

DAYBREAK

Chad arrived back at the search site first. He'd been steadily adding prayers of his own that he would be the one to find his brother that morning. He drove past Chris's house, back down the dirt road, and entered the woods again. It was still frigid, the air brittle and silent around him. He could hear the crackle of his boots as each footfall landed on the crisp ground, but nothing else. It was an eerie stillness he felt in his bones.

His eyes squinted into the dimness. He walked on. Past the private dirt road and entrance into the apple orchard, within yards of the power lines where Chris's phone had last indicated his location. He searched for the sort of cover Chris was known to make for himself during these episodes. Strategic lean-tos that usually featured an ashy campfire within the perimeter.

A gathering of tree limbs tipped him off, and at first, Chad thought his brother was sleeping. He wasn't moving, and there was no sign of harm or worse. He called his name, carefully, knowing it could be dangerous to startle Chris out there. He stepped carefully forward, his eyes never leaving the outline of his brother's body on the ground.

"Chris." Chad moved closer.

"Chris, I'm here." His throat grew tighter, the air hollow and hard through his nose.

"Chris, wake up." His hands reached out to grasp and shake. "Wake up!"

Chad was close enough by then to see a splash of red. Not much, and not everywhere, but enough to know.

The middle brother, Nathan, had just arrived and was suddenly by his side. He asked Chad to confirm what he already knew. Together, they stayed beside Chris, the first and finest hero they'd known, and prayed that he was finally at peace, with God, and relieved of the ceaseless pain he'd battled for too long.

Chad made the most difficult phone call of his life to alert his parents. They'd found Chris.

7:00 AM

Brent and Paula had started the day exhausted from the sleepless night and heavy weight of apprehension, yet hopeful. They drove past Chris's house and down the familiar dirt road that winnowed to a narrow path that led into the woods and power lines, unsure of what this new day would bring. Tumult, for certain, but they both leaned into the hope that Chris's love for his daughters and promise to never do anything to hurt them would be the catalyst—the steadiest beat in his tortured heart—to carry Chris home.

In some ways, perhaps it did.

When they answered Chad's call, and watched two of their three sons emerge from the woods, Brent and Paula felt that hope dissolving into something unyielding and severe.

They would never be whole again.

The darkest night had stolen a piece of them away forever.

The very first piece, the rock-solid middle of their family puzzle, was suddenly gone—and every day since has been an examination of all the ways a pristine border had broken apart.

CHAPTER TWO

1967-1970, THE IT COUPLE

Paula's mother resembled a skier in freefall down a gritty New Hampshire black diamond trail. Her body shot upright and then went slack against the back of the chair. Down she went over the ribbed edge of the oversized cushion, until she was fully splayed out on the floor like a boneless rag doll. Two kids already nervously sweating out the start of a difficult conversation rushed to her aid. The most dramatic announcement of their lives was hitting hard and fast.

—★—

It wasn't fleeting, juvenile, or a particularly potent case of puppy love. Rather, the connection between Brent AuCoin and Paula LeTourneau felt pre-ordained, as though two souls who'd connected on some otherworldly plane had found each other again earthside. Despite the pitfalls and land-mines of high school relationships, Brent and Paula navigated it all with a depth and care for each other that many adults three times their age failed spectacularly to offer. At 14, Paula already knew hardship and pain. She'd lost her father five years prior, and in many ways, lost her mother, too, in the years that followed. Grief and shock can strike so deeply, a person can unspool in no time, and Leona LeTourneau's ability to solo parent after her husband's death was being challenged. She was doing her best to be the provider, working their small insurance company and keeping her daughter safe, well-dressed, and surrounded by nice things, but Leona was not built to be the supportive haven Paula could've used to heal from her own tremendous loss. She was more glamour and fun, adventure and good times, and while Leona loved Paula, she had never truly learned how to be an emotionally present mother—simply because she'd never had one of her own.

As Leona began to construct a new life in the aftermath of tragedy, going out at night and driving around in her convertible with the top down—even in wintertime with the heat blasting—her daughter was forging her own path back to a more conventional happiness. Knowing her mother needed her own space and activities that elevated her new life without her husband, Paula learned to govern her own time and most of it was spent by Brent's side.

Conant High School in Jaffrey, New Hampshire, was tucked into the valley beneath Mount Monadnock in the southwestern corner of the state. When Paula entered for her freshman year, she caught the eye of a certain junior right away. They didn't seek an explanation for this almost instantaneous attraction, nor did they question it—even though a 14 and 17-year-old might attempt to when parents, peers, or siblings offered more seasoned opinions of such young affection. Instead, Paula LeTourneau and Brent AuCoin became inseparable. An unbreakable fusion that forged a steel-like bond. At first, it was fun and adventurous, a newness that felt big, bold, and all-consuming.

If there was an event at Conant High, Brent and Paula attended it together. Their voices mingled in the school choir, and they shared a chairlift when they could during competitions for the ski team. When mutual friends ran into Brent, they asked for Paula. When her friends were around, they wanted to know why Brent wasn't. Both athletic, popular, well-liked, and active in the school community, the freshman and the junior became Conant's closest connection to couple royalty, and inevitably, the first few sparks of a new experience turned into the deeper burn of intimacy and love.

While life felt vast, it also seemed immediate. The future wasn't a then or later for Paula and Brent, it was a here and now. They grew up wrapped in each other's dreams, and in that, made significant plans with the peace of knowing this was it. They had found their forever.

Brent's family embraced Paula with kindness and support. They saw the maturity and dedication of their relationship and were there for Paula when her own mother couldn't be. Her maturation into early adulthood was a patchwork of experiences gleaned from the absence of guidance within her own home, to the steadiness of Brent's. She was a fixture in the AuCoin's day-to-day lives. When Brent was home, Paula was with him. His parents welcomed her presence, but his sister, Pat, doted on her like an older sister would. Pat's husband, Dick, who was seven years older than Brent, also etched out a role for himself that gave Brent the brother he'd never had. As the years went by, Paula grew even closer to Pat—watching her become a wife and mother, and adding another stitch in the patchwork of lessons learned that she would one day use for herself, and a family of her own.

As another September arrived, a new school year would begin, and back to Conant they'd go—eager to assimilate again into the sports and friendship groups they'd left months before. When Brent graduated from high school and attended Keene State College, they began planning in earnest. No topic was taboo, and nothing was off the table. Not even the audacious idea of starting a family right away.

—★—

When the phone rang one morning, Leona was confused to hear the receptionist at their family doctor's office tell her Paula's upcoming appointment had to be moved. "What is this all about?" she demanded from her sixteen-year-old daughter. "Are you sick?"

Paula shook her head and activated the calm demeanor she'd adopted to manage her mother's various moods and reactions. She did a fast and fake workaround explanation that took the sting out of Leona's bewilderment. As soon as her mother walked away, Paula furiously dialed the doctor's office back and constructed a fix.

"This is Paula LeTourneau, and you just called my mom!"

The receptionist heard the desperation in the teenager's voice. "Okay, okay, tell me what's going on."

Paula poured out her predicament. "You gotta fix this!" she ordered.

When the phone rang again, Paula made sure her mother was there to answer.

"Hello," Leona said.

"Oh, Mrs. LeTourneau, hello. This is the receptionist calling again from the doctor's office. I'm so sorry, but I made a mistake. We accidentally confused another patient with Paula. She doesn't have an appointment with us after all. I'm very sorry for the mistake."

Paula sighed in relief. Crisis averted for now, but not for long.

Around the same time, Tena AuCoin, Brent's mother, was looking for something in the glove compartment of Brent's car. In between the registration and a few napkins, her fingers closed around a small three-by-five booklet detailing what to expect in a pregnancy. Instead of going straight to her son, Tena approached Paula. As the second mother confronted Paula about the discovery she'd made in Brent's car, she didn't deny or back pedal. Paula told Tena the truth that would soon become undeniable. Paula was pregnant. The AuCoins wrestled with the realization that their baby was about to be a father while he was still in college—and his girlfriend, even younger! All the worries trickled out during hard conversations and kitchen table heart-to-heart talks: *You're both too young. How can you possibly support a baby? Paula's still in high school. Brent's in college. This won't work!*

Inevitability was a theme in the answers Brent and Paula provided for every question.

"We don't know yet, but we'll figure it out. Somehow, it will all be just fine. Don't worry about us, we love each other and that's all we need."

To them, it was the truth.

Once all the questions were asked and every probability exhausted, Elmer and Tena AuCoin gifted Brent and Paula more than acceptance. They provided a home for them to live in as a couple for the remainder of Paula's pregnancy, and beyond. But first, they had to come clean with Leona. She may not have been the traditionally motherly type that Paula hoped she'd grow into, but two families were about to share a grandchild, and that meant something.

—★—

"Isn't it beautiful?" Leona gushed, proudly displaying the full-length leather coat she'd bought for Paula during a vacation in Spain. "Fancy for fall in New Hampshire, but I couldn't resist. You can wear it in the convertible!"

Paula's stomach was already jumping at the thought of telling her mother she was pregnant, moving in with Brent, and over the moon about it all. Brent had held her hand during the drive from Jaffrey to her mother's home in Rindge. Leona lived on a hundred-acre blend of woods and meadows, and the ride to her house felt interminable. Once inside, the scent of the new leather coat mingled with the stress of their secret, and the fib Paula had told Leona about the doctor's appointment. She had some serious untangling to do.

But first, they had to pick Leona up off the floor.

—★—

Once the shock subsided, Leona rallied Paula's older brother and tried to hatch a plan to "handle" the situation. Paula would travel to England and terminate the pregnancy.

No." The young couple stood firm and final on that plan, and eventually it was vanquished and never spoken of again.

On April 25th, 1970, Paula's brother walked her down the aisle of St. Patrick's Church in Jaffrey and presented her to a misty-eyed Brent, who considered her to be the most beautiful woman in the entire world, and the love of his life. It had taken significant effort to arrange the marriage of a pregnant teenager in the Catholic church. It took Brent and Paula on a journey through the priest of their own church, who'd refused to marry them, to the assistant priest who'd lobbied the Bishop of the Diocese of Manchester, NH. They stubbornly wouldn't give up out of respect for the religious process and the word of the Lord. A church wedding was an expression of God's main commandment, love, and both Brent and Paula believed they would be judged not by their deeds, but by their hearts. When permission was finally granted, they considered themselves blessed and perfectly positioned to overcome any obstacle to come.

Once their marriage was official, Brent and Paula moved into their own place. Well, not their own, per se, but separate from the rest of the AuCoin home—an enclosed front porch big enough for one twin bed and nothing else.

As months went by, Brent was getting closer to graduating from Keene State and Paula's stomach grew and grew. They would lie together at night and imagine what their child would look like. What it would feel like to be parents. How they'd earn enough money to support this new family. They weren't paranoid or frightened, panicked or terrified of missing out on their youth. Brent and Paula AuCoin welcomed everything about to happen to them with gratitude and excitement.

On September 29th, 1970, Christopher Patrick AuCoin arrived. The next day his mother turned 17. Brent and Paula brought their new son home to a renovated loft apartment above his grandparents' garage. They settled into the delight and rigors of caring for a newborn, and life felt about as perfect as they ever imagined it could.

CHAPTER THREE
SAINT CHRISTOPHER

Little Christopher AuCoin was perfect in every way.

Planned, in as much as a teenage mother and her slightly older partner could design a life before aging into full adulthood themselves. Everything they did, every word they spoke, and every dream they dared concoct was rooted in love, family, marriage, and an ironclad promise to overcome whatever challenge arose together. There was nothing the AuCoins couldn't get through, if they were in lock step.

Certainly, life—as it does—tossed out some rough patches. Money was paramount, as Brent and Paula suspected it would be, and carving out enough for their family took sacrifices and induced stress. The loft apartment was tiny, and Chris was growing. They knew they needed more space, but before that could happen, Paula noticed something else that needed more immediate attention.

One day while changing Chris's diaper, she discovered a huge bulge in his lower abdomen. Her stomach tightened and her breath caught as every conceivable ailment poured through her imagination. It was shocking to think anything could be wrong with her pure and flawless little boy, yet Paula didn't hesitate. She stared at the swollen mound for only a short time and then jumped into action. Wrapping Chris in a blanket, she hastily stepped into her shoes and walk-ran two streets over to the doctor's office, where a diagnosis was swiftly declared: Chris had a hernia and would need surgery to repair it.

When that day came, Brent and Paula sat on his parents' front lawn before leaving for the hospital in Keene. They played with Chris, made him laugh and giggle, as much as a distraction for them as him. With silly faces, exaggerated howls, and snorts, two parents danced around the grass working overtime to make this monumental moment in their young son's life less frightful. They would do whatever it took to ensure Chris felt safe and loved. When they handed him off to the surgical team, Brent held Paula by his side, each vibrating with a nervous energy that rolled off them like an electrical spark.

Together. They would get through this together.

Chris came through the surgery like a champ. He never cried, whined, or fussed. But as Paula spent days in the hospital with him as he recovered, she felt the heaviness of raising a child tugging on her like a sinking anchor. While she recognized the inherent risks of life, and had already lost a parent herself, the concept of an ill child had never felt more tangible and real. Suddenly, the fragility of it all hit her. When a little girl of seven or eight years old arrived at the same time Chris was in the pediatric wing, her trachea fractured by a fall into a bedroom bureau, Paula's typically steadfast logic became scrambled. Never one to panic or lose control, seeing children in distress taught her a difficult lesson: accidents can happen, kids can be seriously hurt, and mothers can suffer indescribable pain. She watched over Chris with a heightened alertness born from a love she'd never felt before. It was both heady and intimidating—an instinctual need to protect this little boy with all she had in her.

Which, of course, was an impossible endeavor.

—★—

By 1973, the AuCoin family entered its own space. Bigger than the loft over the garage, yet ancient and worn, they saw potential in an old house in Jaffrey where others noticed rot. If anyone dared warn Brent and Paula about the work it would take to make that place livable, they were met by that classic determination and excitement the young couple was becoming known for. Armed with a thousand-dollar down payment on loan from Pat and Dick, they secured a mortgage for $19,500 and officially became homeowners. On a gray and rainy day, the AuCoins received the keys from the elderly former owner and stepped over the threshold of their new home. Clutching each other, Chris, and cheery visions of Christmas mornings, birthdays, and life milestones about to be had within those walls, they immediately heard what sounded like a waterfall.

"What's that?" Paula turned to Brent. "Water?"

"Oh, it's water, all right," he confirmed, looking up. Brent quickly clocked the source: A stream of rain that was falling from the sky, straight through a massive tear in the roof, and down the stairs to the first floor. He followed it down another level, where water was pooling at an alarming pace in the cellar. Soon, they'd be flooded out down there.

"Seems we have a bit of leak, honey."

It was the sort of understatement they were used to, so Brent and Paula rolled up their sleeves and got to work.

—★—

Chris was a busy three-year-old, energetic yet watchful. He was fascinated by the sounds of saws and hammers, and the smooth feel of fresh planks of two-by-fours they used to reinforce the aged walls. He watched his father and grandparents rebuild every room while Paula tried to keep him warm by the hot air steaming from the worn radiator. She'd tuck his chilled nose into the collar of her sweater as she told stories, explained how houses were built to be strong and sturdy for families like theirs, and all the adventures they'd soon have in their backyard.

"One day soon, you'll have your own bed, in your own room, right up those stairs." She told Chris, pointing to the second floor which still needed attention. Even in its distressed state, she was already thinking the walls of Chris's bedroom should be painted a peaceful blue that would warm with the morning light that faced the horizon. It would be cheerful and dazzling, filled with his favorite stuffed animals, his cozy blankets, and the books she read him to sleep with each night. Eventually, as Chris grew, he chose his own color scheme. It was a whole theme for him. They added red and white to the beautiful blue Paula first chose, a strikingly patriotic wallpaper that was mirrored by a similarly colored quilt Chris requested she make for his bed. Even early on, the colors that represented service and might mattered to Chris, and they filled his most personal space fully.

Room-by-room, the old house's holes were plugged, its rotten boards replaced, all the rusted nails removed and modernized, and the next generation in its history began to lay roots. They welcomed a black lab puppy, who Chris named Pal, minded their finances, and spent what little they could spare on providing their young son with experiences to enrich his soul and expose him to the exquisiteness of the majestic New Hampshire wilderness. Camping, something Chris would one day master, started with a borrowed pop-up, some firewood, and the deep woods of Hampton Beach.

—★—

"Wow," Chris whispered as his eyes went wide, in awe of the soaring pine trees so tall they seemed to pierce right through the puffy clouds above them. They were even taller than his dad, whom he considered to be a giant. When Brent tossed him atop his shoulders and Chris held on to his stubbly chin with one hand, he stretched the other as high as possible, and still, his wiggling fingers couldn't grasp even the lowest limb on the tallest tree.

"Daddy, they're so big!"

The sun was bright in the noontime sky as they reached their camp site at the Tidewater Camping Grounds. The earth was littered with dried brush and skinny needles Chris collected into groupings. Sticks became drawing utensils as they doodled into the silt and sand of the loose dirt. Hours passed. Ladybugs landed on blades of grass, and then climbed on Chris's palm, fascinating him with their gentle motion, and making him giggle as they trotted onto a fingertip. When they flew away, Chris was determined to chase them through the air. His sneakered feet kicked up dusty swirls until each ladybug eventually disappeared into the air around them.

Later, the sun set. Nighttime owls hooted and raccoons skittered about noisily as flames crackled from their campfire, and stars popped out by the dozens. Chris laid his back against his parents' knees and stared at them in wonderment as his mom taught him how to identify clusters, celestial markings, and moonbeams that reflected through the thin layer of clouds. When daylight rose along with the humidity of a summer morning, Chris splashed through puddles left over from a passing rain shower, ate a doughnut he shared with Brent, and deemed it the most wonderful place in all the world.

Right from the beginning, Chris was one with the woods around him. Nestled into the tufts of nature, lulled to sleep by the cricks and croons of native creatures, protected by the lushness of the dark, he felt a harmony of place. He belonged there.

In that luxurious dusk, with an absence of light, Chris reached a homeostasis he would carry with him for the rest of his life—his internal response to a dynamic environment. Stable. Calm. Confident. The leading characteristics of a child who would grow into a competent, accomplished, dependable, loving, and tremendously complicated man.

CHAPTER FOUR
THE GROWING YEARS

The AuCoins were a complete family by the time the 80s rolled around. Chris was joined first by Nathan, and then by Chadwick. Paula and Brent hustled to keep up with their three young sons, and while it was a daily challenge to make ends meet and raise their rambunctious boys, they were filled to the brim with love and pride. This little family was everything they'd talked about, dreamed of, and planned into existence. Life felt full and blessed. Not that there weren't close calls, extreme moments, hard lessons, personal challenges, and difficulties—because there certainly were. Many, in fact. Growing up meant melancholy experiences that built character by forcing those do-the-right-thing moments.

As the oldest child, Chris embraced all the baked-in responsibilities of leadership, lived by example, and passed along the necessity of hard work. At just 8 years old, he turned an interest in horses into a job and assigned roles to every member of his family. His Shetland pony, Fern, was on loan from a stable in a nearby town—which meant Chris could assume all the care duties in a shared relationship with the pony's owner, whose own sons had outgrown their roles. The excitement spilled over into Chris assigning ranch hand jobs for everyone: Paula was the cook, while his grandfather,

father, and two brothers were the ranch hands. A proper setup for a pony was established at the AuCoin house, complete with a list of everything Fern would need when she came to stay with them.

"Dad, we'll need a stall." Chris's hair fluttered around his forehead as his eyes moved from the list he was making to his parents' amused faces. It was an entire family effort, and they were pleased to see how immersed Chris was in taking the lead. "Fern needs a stall. And hay, too."

"She'll need grain along with that hay, Chris," Paula told him. "Horses need a lot of both. And she'll need to be walked every day."

"Yes! I know, Mom. I'll do that."

Brent and Paula exchanged a glance. Chris was falling hard for Fern, and it was a relationship that would be both the sweetest and one of the most painful of his young life so far.

—★—

"Let's get her tail all jazzed up!" Paula was with Chris inside the ten-by-ten stall they'd built for Fern on their property, which boasted plenty of space and wide-open acres to let the boys run wild. Fern spent endless hours beneath summer sunshine prancing around on a lead, Chris holding the leather strap carefully to exercise her properly while keeping her safe within a contained boundary. With her dapple-gray body and silvery blonde mane and tail, Fern was a stunner, and Paula was helping Chris braid red, white, and blue ribbons into her flowy locks and swooshy tail.

"She'll be the prettiest pony in the entire Memorial Day parade," Chris told his mom with a firm nod. "I know she will."

At that time, Chris fancied himself a fine cowboy and eventual ranch owner. He gathered all the necessary accoutrements: chaps, the iconic ten-gallon hat, a toy gun and holster, and boots with real spurs, and stepped into all of them for the big town gathering. Everyone would be there, and Fern would dazzle them all.

Behind the floats and somewhere in between the marching bands and clown car, Chris proudly sat upon Fern's back, gripping the reins in between his fingers to gently tug her bit to stop, slow, or move along. She was perfect that day. Her thick braids danced along with her steady gait, she whinnied at the adoring crowd and responded perfectly to every correction Chris gave her. He pushed his hat higher on his crown to ensure an unimpeded view of all the people lining the street. He wanted to make every single one of them snapped to attention when he and Fern trotted by. Not for him so much as the trusty pony he'd grown to love. She deserved to know how much she meant to him, and their entire town.

Chris kept such a close and careful watch on his girl that even the smallest alteration to her routine concerned him. He was out in the yard with her one day, as he was most days, but something about Fern was… off.

"Mom!" Chris came running into the house where Paula was helping Nathan find a shoe and keeping Chad from snapping in half all his brother's crayons. Like usual, it was controlled chaos.

"Mom! Where are you, Mom?"

Paula left the closet with instructions for Nate to go check for the shoe under his bed and swung through the living room where she plucked a still whole lavender crayon from between Chad's tiny fingers.

"Chad, I said no. Do not break your brother's crayons!"

"Mom!"

"Chris, stop yelling, I'm right here. What's going on?"

"There's something wrong with Fern," he told her with wide eyes and small droplets of sweat merging into a river that ran over one eyebrow. He blinked away the moisture. "Come, please. Come outside with me right now!"

Paula scooped Chad onto her hip, and yelled up to Nathan—who was loudly removing items from beneath his bed in search of his wayward shoe—and followed Chris outside.

"Honey, please don't run. I have your brother here. Chris! Wait for me!"

Chris dashed ahead. He felt an odd current of energy that tingled his fingertips and made his stomach queasy. He would later associate that feeling with worry and fear about something he considered precious. Fern, to him, was everything—right up there with his mom, dad, and brothers. Fern was family.

Paula also felt sweat beading on her forehead. As she tried to keep up with Chris and managed the extra weight of her sturdy child on her hip, she folded her hand along her brow to block out the sun and find Chris far ahead. He was at the fence line yet had eased himself through the rails to where Fern was standing. Paula slowed her pace and squinted.

"See, Mom? See? Fern's sick!"

But was she truly sick? Paula tilted her head and did a fast sweep of Fern from nose to hoof. *Hmmmph.* Chris was right. Fern's long neck was angled down like an arrow, her bright mane splayed around her eyes, and her mouth nearly level with the ground. She was standing, but appeared somewhat wobbly. Something was indeed wrong, but Paula wasn't sure what it could be.

"Okay, honey," she started, quickly running through her options. She was home alone with the boys, Brent was at work, she wasn't up to speed on potential pony health complications, and Chris was deeply worried. She had to do something, and fast.

"Let's go inside, sweetheart. I'm going to make a phone call and see if we can figure out what's going on with Fern."

Chris felt that odd rustling of nerves scampering across his chest again as he watched Paula dial the number for a local rancher she knew. He paced around the floor with his hands tightly bound in front of his waist. The drying sweat on his face left whitish streaks down his cheeks. He couldn't help but loud whisper to her even as she was trying to listen to instructions over the phone.

"What's he saying, Mom? Tell me! What's wrong with Fern?"

Paula put a finger to her lips to hush Chris so she could hear the rancher.

"Oh," she said, as surprise widened her eyes. "Oh, my. Oh, yes, yes, I'll go check on that right now."

She placed the phone back on the cradle, told Chris to hurry along behind her, left Chad on the floor with a strict warning to not touch a single crayon while she was gone, yelled up to the second floor for Nate to come watch his brother, and rushed back out the door with Chris.

"The rancher wants us to check something," she told Chris in mid-step.

"Okay, Mom. Check what?"

Paula could see every inch of her yard in her head but wanted visual real-world confirmation. She headed back out to where Fern was still oddly bent over. The rancher had asked her a pointed question: *"Do you have apple trees on your property? Was Fern able to access them?"*

Paula kept moving beyond the fence and toward the section of her big yard where a row of apple trees grew tall and proud from seedlings planted long before they'd moved in. Every fall, she and the boys collected the ruby red balls to make pies and crisps. She saw the trees and a slew of fallen orbs scattered along the ground.

"Oh, no!" she blurted out, temporarily forgetting to temper her response to avoid launching Chris into a full-blown panic. Too late.

"What, Mom? WHAT?!"

Paula twisted at the torso, trying to focus on Fern and her harried son at the same time. First, she'd calm Chris and then attend to the pony—who, according to the rancher, was exhibiting signs of being overserved.

"Honey, Fern is going to be okay, but I have to get her back to the stall." She reached down and grabbed one of the wormy apples that appeared to have been crunched through by large square teeth. "See here? Fern has been eating a lot of these rotting apples that fall from our trees. They're making her sick. But, Chris, I promise she's going to be all right. Just… no more apples for now."

Chris's mouth twisted as his mind worked to compute what his mother was telling him. He often gave Fern apples straight from his palm and she happily gobbled them up. "But, but, Mom, Fern eats apples all the time," he reasoned. "I give her apples! Is it my fault she's sick?"

Paula winced. The last thing she wanted was for Chris to assume responsibility for Fern's condition. "No, not at all. It's not anybody's fault. It's not Fern's fault either."

And then she went on to explain to her young son what it meant to be drunk. Because their sweet little pony was indeed drunk on fermented apples.

From then on, Chris put himself on rotten apple patrol and swept them away before Fern could eat herself plastered again.

"We're not going to let Fern get drunk ever again." Once Chris took up a position, he stood by it.

Fern would never be apple bombed on his watch.

—★—

Even though Fern was Chris's first true love, and he protected her as such, other loves came along and after a few years the AuCoins realized Fern needed more attention than they could give her. Chris was on his dirt bike more than he was in the field with his pony, and while he would always adore Fern, he knew it was time to send her back. They called her owner, kissed her goodbye as she was loaded into the trailer, and brushed away tears that swelled from their sad eyes. Growing up wasn't easy, nor was being mature enough to accept when something wonderful had run its course. Fern had been a magical part of Chris's upbringing, and to this day, anytime Paula and Brent hear the song *Wildfire* by Michael Martin Murphey, all those happy memories flood in.

A sweet, dappled pony, the gentle ways Chris took care of her, and the remarkable connection they'd shared. He'd made the right choice for Fern, even though it hurt to let her go.

Raising children in the country, with long windy dirt roads, giant oak trees to climb, streams to plunder, and hills to conquer generated early dexterity, physical awareness, strong leadership, and sometimes… trouble.

—★—

While the AuCoin homestead supplied ample space for the boys to explore, there were neighbors nearby, and the boys played together often.

Humid summer afternoons were spent traversing the land, making swords out of sticks, defending the misshapen rock they deemed a pirate ship from invaders, digging worms from the crusty earth and winding them through fingers, or anything young minds could come up with. And in that, things can often go haywire.

"Hello?" Paula said into the phone. She'd fed the boys sandwiches for lunch and sent Chris back out to play with some neighborhood friends. Often, he'd be gone for hours, and it occurred to her she hadn't seen him in a while. Chris loved being outside and could keep himself busy without pestering her to entertain him. Paula loved that about her oldest son, he was independent and capable. That's why all the air in her lungs got stuck when she heard who was calling, and why.

"I'm bringing Chris home." His friend's mother informed her. Paula choked on that air with what she told her next. "And you should get him to the doctor right away."

Sometimes, an inch or two can make all the difference between tragedy and triumph. A lightning strike that misses a gathering of baseball players on a diamond by mere feet, or a hunch to pause before driving to the store—then later learning a four-car crash happened just around the time you would have pulled up to that intersection. In Chris's case that summer, he got the bad odds and took an acorn straight to the eye.

Paula fast walked in a circle from the kitchen to the living room and front door, waiting for Chris to be delivered back home. Both Nate and Chad watched her, getting the sense that something was wrong, and their mom was acting strange. Nervous. She kept her voice low to avoid scaring her boys, but Paula's heart was pounding out of her chest, and her mouth had gone bone dry. Her imagination was whipping up disastrous scenarios and horrifying injuries—but whatever they were about to deal with, she would handle it once she could see, touch, and hug Chris.

The neighbor's car turned into the driveway.

Paula heard the crunch of tires and sprinted to the door. She held her breath and swung it open, a little dizzy and unsteady. *Please,* she whispered. *Please let Chris be okay.*

"Paula, I didn't see it, but the boys told me what happened," the neighbor began, but Paula wasn't hearing words. She could only stare in horror at Chris's face.

His eye!

Paula talked herself down from a messy reaction and maintained that calm composure Chris expected and needed from her in that frightening moment. She noticed he wasn't crying or panicking and was already apologizing for causing a fuss.

"I'm sorry, Mom. We didn't mean to. It was just an accident."

It was a fingertip-sized acorn the boys were throwing around, which – in that unlucky way the universe can sometimes maneuver events– managed to ricochet itself off the side of a barn and directly into Chris's eye. By the time he returned home, it had turned a feral amber, bright like an animal's eye would be in the haze of moonlight.

—★—

"We'll need to admit him," the doctor explained as he examined Chris's injured eye.

Brent and Paula sat together in the hospital once again, worried about Chris, leaning on and physically against each other as they absorbed a dire warning that his sight could be lost in that eye if it hemorrhaged again.

"And strict bed rest for a while. We can't risk a bleed."

They nodded at the doctor and understood what could happen. During Chris's hospital stay, his absence hit deeply at home. Little brothers missed their big brother so much they insisted on being next to him. As in climbing into the same tiny hospital bed. They'd scoot around Chris's longer legs and sturdy midsection to find space along his side. Nate would tuck himself around Chris's pointy elbow and lean his chin up to see the bandage wrapped around half his brother's face.

"Don't touch it, Nate. I don't want your creepy crawly germs all over me." Chris was firm but Nate always wiggled around all his hard big brother edges.

"Touch, touch, touch," he sang, tapping his finger against Chris's nose.

"You're a pain!"

"No, you're a pain!"

So it went for the duration of Chris's eye recovery. His brothers teased and poked, but Nate wouldn't stay away from Chris's bed, even when he came home. It was as though the only way through this traumatic family event for the middle brother was being able to feel Chris by his side and hear him whisper, *I'm okay, Nate,* before he fell asleep every night.

The seriousness of his injury kept Chris under doctor's orders for a while, but because he was mature and patient beyond his years, his eye fully recovered, and normal life resumed.

Until the next thing.

The AuCoins were learning to roll with the punches three sons can deliver.

—★—

"Nope. No. Absolutely not!"

Paula's mouth formed a tight line as she was peppered by her husband, father-in-law, and 13-year-old Chris.

"But Mom, you know I'm responsible. I'm a teenager now!"

Chris cajoled her like a pro. He said all the right things and despite the acorn and a bunch of cuts, scrapes, broken bones, and stitches he'd racked up, was very grown-up for his age. Paula knew in her mother's heart that Chris never lied, cheated, or failed to watch out for his brothers.

But, really? A dirt bike?

"Mom, come on. We're just going to go look at some. That's all."

On the ride over to the bike dealership in Swansey, New Hampshire, Brent mulled it over. Sure, Chris was smart and capable. He was also starting to feel his teenage oats and loved adventure. He was responsible and level-headed, a good student, and a big help with the boys at home. Brent was more willing to be convinced than his wife, that was for sure, but when Chris spotted *the one,* Pepe made the call to grab it then and there, and Chris came home to his mother with a brand-new dirt bike and a sly grin. "Pepe said I could have it."

When Paula tucked the boys into bed that night, she squatted low beside Chris's bed to look him square in the eye. This moment needed to stick.

"First, you're a very lucky boy to have something like that, but second of all, you can hurt yourself or someone else if you are not careful with that bike. I mean careful *all… the …time."* She slowly enunciated each word and stared into Chris's wide eyes. "Don't make me worry about you, Chris. Okay?"

Chris shifted on his elbows and put his back against the pillows to gain some height.

"Okay," he responded, his eyes now level with Paula's. Chris wanted to be authoritative like a man but heard his voice crack, still figuring out how not to sound like a little kid. Intuitively, Chris realized his mom needed this to be a sentinel intersection in their relationship. On that night, in that talk, he knew she was letting go even though it was killing her. He had to respect what that must feel like.

"I promise. I'll be careful."

Paula nodded and accepted his word.

Chris always kept his word.

She got used to seeing him dart off, helmet firmly secured to his head, down the back roads and pebbly paths that formed between houses in their neighborhood. Chris was among many boys his age with a dirt bike, and by and large, they were careful enough. Funny, even.

Like the time they were out climbing berms and spinning their tires as they slunk down beneath low tree limbs. Paula could see the group outside her window and watched as a Jaffrey Police Department cruiser pulled into the empty lot near their house. *What was that about,* she wondered.

"Come on, boys, let's take a walk."

Nate and Chad tumbled out of the front door and raced toward where the action was—which was always where Chris and the big kids were. Paula squinted. She could see the uniformed officer exit his patrol car and walk over to where the boys were gathered, their legs astride bike seats to hold them steady against the ground. Both little brothers ran ahead of her, but given there was an officer of the law present, Paula didn't worry too much about either finding mischief. Her gaze narrowed on the officer and the teenagers on bikes, wondering what had brought him out there, and what he was talking to them about. She was so intently focused on trying to read their lips, she didn't notice Chad scoot by the open cruiser door and jump right into the driver's seat!

Oh, jeesh. Paula swung her gaze to see her son's body swallowed inside the front of the cruiser.

"Chad!" she yelled, racing over, cupping her arms beneath his armpits, and yanking him out. "Oh my gosh, Officer, I'm so sorry! He got away from me for a minute."

The loudest laugh came from Chris, who found great humor in watching his little brothers do crazy things.

And when Chris became an altar boy in the same church where his parents were married, both Nate and Chad watched him perform his duties from a row near the front of the church. They tried to distract Chris, make him laugh or lose his composure, but the biggest brother never wavered. He was always calm, cool, and competent. Which was why, when a disturbing call came in from "Sister L" at the St. Patrick Catholic Church school in which Chris was enrolled, the AuCoins were stunned.

—★—

Brent and Paula learned the alleged crime involved a peach. Sister L led a school-wide effort to castigate, humiliate, and demean Chris for taking a peach from his lunch tray and, to garner a laugh from his friends, pretend he was going to stuff it into a girl's back pocket on her jeans. Cafeteria supervisors saw the incident unfold, alerted Sister L, and hauled Brent and Paula before the school principal. They were already projecting Chris's future off this one silly incident, and it was a grim outlook.

"Mr. and Mrs. AuCoin," Sister L began, her face serious and glum. "Your son has obvious impulse control issues, is highly inappropriate in public settings, and we fear…" she trailed off with the horror of the label she was about to assign to their son. She looked at the principal, who shared the same pathetic visage of disappointment and dread.

"You fear what, Sister?" Brent pushed. He and Paula were already annoyed at the blatant dramatization of the peach event, and while they would speak to Chris about being more temperate with girls and do better to avoid seeking the title of class clown, they also knew this was an absurd overreach. "What exactly are you saying?"

Sister L's dour face was pinched, her lips forming an upside-down letter 'u.' Paula's fingers sat in her lap, rubbing themselves raw as she waited for her to drop a hammer on them. She felt anxious, but mostly angry, with a slow burn rising from her stomach, past her heart, and into the back of her throat. She felt the heat in her cheeks. *Just say it already,* she told Sister L without speaking. Just say it!

"Well, it pains me deeply," Sister L spat. Her eyes took a circular route from the principal, to Brent, and then to Paula. "I take no joy in this, please understand that, but I am very concerned Chris could one day become a bridge sitter."

Now, to fully understand the impact of that assessment, an awareness of local lore was imperative. Around Jaffrey, New Hampshire, the notion of becoming a *bridge sitter* meant losing yourself to a hardened, lonely, often crime-riddled existence. The bridge sitters were the town's losers, who stared down through rusted out metal bars at rocky shores and mucky water, absent from society, and holding no real value to themselves or anyone else, lost and depressed—unproductive and unloved.

Vagrants.

Drifters.

Failures.

Brent felt Paula's body go taut just as his own fists clenched in his lap. A bridge sitter? How dare they!

After that day, it became clear to Brent, Paula, and even Chris that the environment at St. Patrick's Catholic Church school wasn't a good fit for him. While he loathed complaining, and rarely indulged in even uttering a grievance, there were events piling up that he simply could no longer bear. Clutching a screwdriver in his palm one night after dinner, he sat across from Brent and Paula at the kitchen table and recounted a particularly horrific punishment for having a mild disagreement with another boy at recess.

Brent watched his son twist the screwdriver, hot tears burning behind his eyes, hating how he felt: Humiliated, dehumanized, belittled.

"Just say it, Chris, what happened?" Brent coaxed. He saw that even relaying the event was eating at Chris.

"They held a mock trial," he began, his face going from pink to crimson. "I was on trial. The criminal."

Paula couldn't help the sharp gasp, and she quieted herself by placing two fingers over her mouth. "Go on."

"Sister R was the judge. Each kid in my class was a witness."

"Uh-hmm." Brent prodded again but was becoming livid and feared he would burst out regrettable words if he widened his mouth.

"I was interrogated," Chris went on. "Asked questions about what I did." He paused, but the screwdriver kept twisting. Round it went inside his grip. "But then, Sister R asked them to do something else."

Paula's heart sank. How could this get any worse?

"What, Chris? What did she ask them to do?"

The screwdriver stopped moving. Chris's head lowered. He was ashamed, becoming smaller, making a physical retreat to some safe place inside himself. He took a deep breath, held, and released it. He looked up at his parents, his eyes hooded with devastation.

"She asked them to say to the whole class what they thought of me. Every classmate got to say their opinion of me. Out loud. For everyone to hear."

That was the last day Chris ever stepped foot inside St. Patrick's Catholic Church school.

When Chris graduated from Merrimack High School, having thrived in a public-school setting, all those early attributes were cemented: honesty, steadiness, loyalty, kindness, and dependability. But something else had stirred as Chris had grown up, endured indignancy, tasted success, encountered difficulties, and launched his own thorough personal assessments of the kind of man he wanted to be. He saw the world more clearly, and what his place in it should be. Maybe it all started with the feeling he had on Fern's back, her mane braided with all the colors of the flag, proudly representing the meaning of the holiday together. Or perhaps it was the injustice of sitting in a chair, embroiled in insufferable cheap shots and a nun's mean-spirited effort to unravel his self-confidence and strip him of his innate goodness. Or, as Brent and Paula believed, it was simply who Chris was from the day he was born.

A warrior.

When he told them, for a second time, he had enlisted in the Marines, they weren't shocked. Instead, they did what every military parent has done for as long as sons and daughters have answered the call to carry out their nation's mission to protect and serve.

They listened.

They supported their son in every way they could.

And they prayed.

A lot.

CHAPTER FIVE
UN-LISTED

Technically, Chris enlisted in the Marines twice. Brent and Paula pulled the parent card the first time, when Chris dropped the shocking news during his senior year in high school. Dinner that night took a hard turn.

"You did what?!" Brent's knees slammed against the wooden slats of their table, rattling metal cutlery and sloshing liquid from glasses.

Chris was nonplussed, although he kept his eyes locked on his fork as it snagged a piece of Paula's baked chicken. He popped the bite into his mouth and chewed. He was aware his announcement was not what his parents were prepared to hear, given they had other plans for Chris, but he'd known for some time that college wasn't for him. At least not then. A larger purpose, to Chris, wasn't some existential platitude often used to charm and ingratiate the curious into signing their youth away. No, to Chris, it felt pre-determined—as though his body and mind had intentionally grown in such a way to meet the challenge head-on.

He swallowed the chicken, took a mouthful of water to wash it down, cleared his throat, and repeated his intentions.

"I enlisted in the Marines today."

This time it was Paula who chose logic to quell the rising heat of this unexpectedly tempestuous family discussion.

"But, Chris," she began, "Honey, you're not old enough to join the Marines. You must finish high school, and then maybe we can talk about this."

"No."

Chris's simple response landed like a boot on brick: hard and final. Brent and Paula were suspended in a strange time warp. They couldn't take back or erase what they'd just heard and yet they couldn't allow it to continue. This was crazy! Chris was seventeen years old! Nate and Chad, usually a chorus of wise cracks and taunts, were silent as they watched their older brother masterfully challenge his parents with just one word.

Brent rolled his palm over his knuckles and stared at Chris's tight mouth, thinking to himself how different his boy suddenly appeared. That notorious switch every father knew would one day turn on, had just been flipped. His son had rocketed from a tentative little towhead testing boundaries, to a block of a teenager chiseled by dedicated hours in the high school weight room, and bold enough to make his own choices. Chris was a man.

And yet he wasn't. Brent still had to protect him.

From himself.

At least for a few more months anyway.

—★—

The Early Enlistment Program, or Delayed Entry Program (DEP), the AuCoins learned, was an opportunity for high school students to enlist prior to graduation and postpone training until their affairs were in order. To Chris, it was the first plank he'd use to build his future, and by signing his name on a document it seemed final—yet, there was an out built in for instances such as this—when a young man's parents deem the decision inappropriate, naïve, and dangerous. The Marines did not take that lightly, and neither did Major Dade.

He did not smile or make small talk when the AuCoins showed up at his Portsmouth office to officially bounce Chris from the United States Marine Corps. Even Leona had joined them that day, to support not only Brent and Paula, but her grandson, too, whom she knew was highly disappointed, embarrassed, and despondent with this forced early exit from the Corps.

"Remind me," Major Dade began, his hardened face stony, lips sucked around the corners of his mouth in a sneer. "Remind me why you're here."

He likely knew exactly what he was dealing with yet refused to be gentle when a viable candidate was being ripped away in an exchange for a cozier life. He didn't have time for that, and worse, no patience or understanding for helicopter parenting.

Chris stood before this imposing man and met his eyes as Major Dade told the AuCoins they were making a huge mistake. When they failed to acquiesce and allow Chris to pursue a career in the Marines, Major Dade then deemed them unpatriotic.

That stung.

They returned home and tried to distract Chris by encouraging him to get his real estate license, as Leona had decades ago. He did just that and joined his grandmother for an internship that prepared him for the New Hampshire real estate market, finding his first clients, and understanding the process of buying and selling homes. Brent and Paula believed, at that time, Chris was the only high school senior in the state to have his real estate license. They were proud of his grit, impressed by his ability to change course, and figured he'd worked that military longing out of his system. Chris graduated from high school, turned eighteen years old, and appeared to be well-positioned to swiftly rise in the premiere real estate circles of the highest earners. A burgeoning mover and shaker!

—★—

"I have some news."

Dinnertime at the AuCoin house was often the only time they had together to catch up and talk. Brent had moved the family from his hometown of Jaffrey to a more central New Hampshire town for a job at Digital Equipment Corporation, or DEC. Computer technology was booming, and Brent's engineering resume plugged certain holes the company needed to fill. But the job was demanding, and Brent spent a significant time away from home. He listened intently to the boys during their family dinners, trying to absorb every word, facial expression, and goofy story so he could replay them during lonely nights in faraway hotel rooms to maintain a connection to the family he missed.

Nate and Chad would share whatever was going on at school, while Brent asked questions and Paula filled in the specifics. He would also share stories of places he'd been. It was a sacred family tradition, and given how many weeks out of the year Brent spent away, Paula considered the nights he was home, and all the boys gathered around the table, truly precious. She also had that mother's sense when something was brewing in any of her sons. That night, she was focused on Chris.

"Go ahead, honey, what's your news?" she asked him, yet wasn't sure she was ready for what he'd say.

Chris approached this dinnertime talk with his family differently than those that had come before. He didn't declare so much as inform, that respect for his parents' wishes still present, but in the backseat now that he was of legal age. From that night forward, Chris was driving, and the most important decisions in his life would be all his to make.

"I joined the Marines. For real this time."

That switch Brent felt go off inside of him flickered again. While it may have been stuck somewhere in between all this time, Chris was telling them it was now and forever in the 'on' position. He had taken over his own life and would do with it as he pleased. And the Marines, for better or worse, were back in control.

The blow was softened a little when Chris explained he'd joined the USMC Reserves, which meant he would eventually be stationed in Manchester, New Hampshire. First, he would undergo intense training to become proficient and worthy. That meant the AuCoins had to say goodbye.

—★—

The summer of 1990 was muggy and warm, but particularly hot the day a Marine recruiter knocked on their door. Polite, formal, and all business, the recruiter had come to accompany Chris to boot camp. Brent, Paula, Nate, and Chad were instructed to bid Chris farewell in the house, while the recruiter waited outside. It was not a request, they understood, but a final moment of privacy they were being granted as a courtesy. Arms linked together, chests up and proud, the family hugged Chris—the rock—and whispered messages directly into his ear, so that only he would know what was heaviest on each of their hearts.

Weeks passed. Paula often spoke to Chris in the open air of her kitchen, preparing dinner for a table that felt uncomfortably smaller. Nate and Chad found more time for themselves in the shared bathroom with one less brother waiting in line to brush his teeth, but mostly they wiled away hours thinking of what Chris was going through, what they'd say when they saw him again, and if he'd ever tell them what it was like to be a Marine. Brent carried on with work, which was demanding even more of his time. He was always on the move, traveling across the country and oceans, putting out fires and strategizing next steps for a company experiencing growing pains and dependent on his expertise and forward thinking.

The hours spent in the air travelling to put out work embers provided ample time for reflection. Brent thought of the strain his job put on Paula, who'd taken jobs here and there to supplement the family budget, but otherwise was often the sole parent available for each son. How he missed them terribly when he was away and had noticed lately how difficult it was becoming for him to focus more on his work tasks and less on home. On Paula. On Nate and Chad.

And a lot on Chris. The young man had shown sparks of an entrepreneurial spirit through his teenage years, washing pots and pans at Lagana's

Meat and Deli Shop until the owner took note of his work ethic and elevated him to potato salad maker and counter service. When he got his driver's license and his grandmother, Tena, gifted him her orange Ford pickup, already high in miles from family trips to Maine, Chris drove it with great care. The truck traversed New Hampshire highways and back roads, carrying Chris from the deli to his eventual new job at Diver's Den in Manchester, where the owners took a shine to Chris after he'd obtained his scuba diving certification. From customer to assistant manager, Chris worked for the Kurisko family right through high school graduation—and developed a deep love for the peaceful depths of the northeast's beautiful waterways. After convincing Chad to also get his diver's certification, the two explored the rocky shores and sandy coastlines of New Hampshire and Maine, ducking beneath the cool waves of the Piscataqua River in Portsmouth, scouring for ancient artifacts near Nubble Light House in York, Maine. Chris regaled customers at Diver's Den with these stories, his eyes aglow with the magic of releasing pieces of clay and metal from their frozen lock of another time, lost to the current and the darkness of countless ebony winters. Chris's love and appreciation for the water evolved through his life and would often call to him during the riotous years to come.

For all those reasons and more, Brent and Paula put their trust in faith while Chris served his country.

Faith that Chris was stepping into who he was always meant to be.

Faith that he would be safe.

And faith that their family would remain intact.

CHAPTER SIX
DEFENSIVE POSITION

Buddy Hackett had heard of Chris in the reserve unit before he'd met him in person, and the physical presentation made him do a double take. Built like a muscle-bound New England lumberjack, and on that day, dressed in bibs, a brown t-shirt, and a black cap, Buddy examined the one guy who resembled a stacked body builder sticking out in a group of ten who stood before him in the DSA (Division Support Area) in Saudi Arabia.

"Who the fuck are you?" he demanded of Chris, then threw his arm wide to include the group. "Yo, guys, who is this farmer?"

Chris took a sip of water from his canteen, neither disturbed nor aggrieved. "I'm Aucoin."

Buddy huffed. "Acorn? So, you're a farmer *and* a nut?"

Not the most elegant of introductions given the acorn incident that almost stole Chris's eyesight, but from that day forward, Buddy wanted to be near Chris for everything they'd encounter in the desert of the Middle East, participating in a war but feeling like they were being left to their own devices to figure out how to survive it.

—★—

Buddy was only a year or two older than Chris, but over there, age dictated status. Throughout the decades of friendship that followed, Chris refused to call Buddy anything other than his title. It simply wasn't proper to do otherwise.

"Corporal?" Chris started one night during guard duty to monitor a road to nowhere that occasionally delivered foreign military passing through. Buddy was patient, and the hours on duty together with Chris were long. He'd noticed that Chris weighed his words and spoke slowly, thoughtfully, as if measuring the value of his input before offering it.

"Ya?"

"I'm not sure what to do after."

"After this shithole?"

"Yes. After."

Buddy noisily dragged in some air that always tasted like oil and gunk. He also took a moment to think about his response. Chris was always watching him, calculating questions he respected him too much to ask. Steady and silent, Chris wasn't a talker, more of a maneuverer, and *man,* was he competent. When Buddy would deliver things back to his unit, items like pics, shovels, or an ax they could hook into a Humvee, telling them the Tooth Fairy had dropped them off, Chris's eyes examined the loot, his hands cupped his hips, but his mind whirled. What he really wanted was the story. The *where.* The *how.*

Where did you get this? And how?

Buddy would occasionally grab a few of the guys to visit their local Army friends and relieve them of their excess. He'd quickly learned his group of Marine reservists was among the finest men he'd ever known, a blend of cops, firefighters, and others of solid character. Yet, when they were all activated for Operation Desert Storm and assembled onto the same platoon and squad, they were outfitted with next to nothing, left-overs, rationed food and water, and hand-me-downs.

Buddy's late-night runs were creative ways to get his boys more stuff. Chris wanted in on that boldness and creativity. To learn how to use his mind, courage, and ingenuity to take care of himself and anyone under his watch. When Buddy spoke of the future with Chris that night, it was honest, yet measured. Because he was never sure, moment to moment, whether they'd ever get out of the desert at all.

—★—

Kuwait. Scorching sun and excruciating temperatures. 110 degrees during the day. Theirs was a cold weather unit, trained to survive in brutally frigid conditions, and yet, that expertise was lost to sweat and struggle in the barren dust bowl. The allied forces made fast progress on the ground, yet bunker systems built in the sand layers just beneath the earth needed to be secured. Small holes in the ground that were littered with booby traps, and trip wires attached to grenade pins, rank with diesel fuel saturated into the walls, the tunnels were a high stakes gamble. Valuable intel may be recovered, or a body could be blown to bits by an unsuspecting footfall on a trigger.

Buddy was down in the belly of one of the tunnels, surrounded by concrete walls and dank air. Every hundred feet or so, he'd glance up at a sliver of light and expand his nostrils to grab outside air being fed into the tunnel through a small pipe. His hands gripped the stiff ridges of his AK with a folding stock, his boots kicking through trash and belongings left behind by fleeing Iraqis. His light cut streams of illumination through black shadows and corners. It was both terrifying and what was deemed necessary to do.

Clear the area.

He steadied his breathing, turned around, and hightailed it back to the entrance. Light, dimmed by the sheen of burning oil over the sun, splashed around the round entrance of the tunnel. Buddy saw a group forming, higher ranking Marines and others.

And there was Chris. Steady. Watching him to make sure he was okay.

Buddy stood at the entrance of the secret bunker where Iraqis had eaten, slept, and plotted. They would have tortured and killed an American intruder as swiftly as taking their own next breath. In that, Buddy needed a beat.

Chris stood before him and took stock. He took off his own t-shirt, spat into it, and wiped the sweat off Buddy's face, succinct and purposeful in his actions.

"You good?"

Buddy nodded. "Yeah."

"Okay, then. Let's get outta here."

Buddy gave Chris the lead right then. He followed Chris away from the tunnel's opening and in the years that followed, he would realize they were both in shock that day—many days, not fully disconnected from what was happening around them, but almost marginalizing or diminishing it enough so it could fit into the emotionally esoteric box of combat. They never had explicit instructions on how to do anything over there, but Chris never balked, wavered, or failed—even when he wasn't sure what the hell was happening.

Which was quite often.

—★—

Kevin Sullivan also joined the Marines at eighteen years old. He was on that military family fast track by the time he met Chris in the reserves. Married with two kids, his wife pregnant with their third, he and Chris didn't have much in common back then, just a joint mission command structure and an unyielding determination to survive so they could get back home to New Hampshire.

Food was scarce, clean water a rarity. As Iraqi forces retreated from Kuwait, they left a hellscape behind. Hundreds of oil wells were purposely set ablaze in a wickedly vengeful act against the earth and the forces sent to beat the Iraqi occupation back. For months, time held no value as the daytime sky turned black with soot, and night glowed with open air flames leaping into the sky. The buzz of oil gushing from sabotaged wells mixed with the crackle of fire—an insufferable combination of sounds none of them could escape.

"Sull!" Chris's voice sounded strangled as it cut through the smoky air. Every soldier was losing vocal range, tonsils and throats coated with contaminants and pollution.

"Yo!"

"I tell you to go, you high tail your ass outta there, man. You got me?"

Chris's head was on a swivel at every moment, and he watched Kevin's position and flank. But the task was enormous, because Chris—as the machine gunner in the platoon's protection services—kept watch over *every* Marine. It haunted him. 100 percent containment was the only acceptable outcome even as the platoon of young men marched across minefields laid by battle hardened Iraqi soldiers, hungry for American casualties.

"You take out anything you have to!"

It was a standing order, to kill whatever popped up in front of you.

Their life, or yours, Marine.

No day, only night, and vague instructions to capture and contain Iraqi soldiers for transport, gather their weapons and load them onto trucks. The Iraqis outnumbered the Marines by the thousands, and if it came to an ambush, there was nothing much to do but fire out the load of any gun you had, and then… go out swinging. It was an iron umbrella mentality that hung over them.

Even though the horizon had disappeared in the toxic smog, they still scanned for enemy vehicles or stragglers with deadly weapons. They prowled and snarled, like animals contained in a noxious cage and prepared to die in a host of merciless ways. As they lived with that awareness, the Marines, and Chris grew to understand hunger, thirst, and being afraid. One of the biggest fears of all: an invisible, insidious blossom of poison the military developed a warning system to guard against—and that alarm went off constantly.

—★—

Phil Smith dreamed of being a pilot, and a Marine. In 1990, he was in the reserves doing his flight work, the final stretch of a prolific military resume that included years of active duty, including special operations. When Manchester, New Hampshire's Bravo company was called up, despite being the cold weather mountain unit that it was, Phil was also part of the group that reported to the desert.

Marines can be colorful, Phil knew, especially the younger ones. Yet the strapping man he grew to count on to get something done without any flack was quiet, calculated, and owned the first hand that always went up to volunteer for a task. When they were warned of the biohazards in the air, it mattered to Chris especially that every Marine was prepared. His 100 percent containment, laser-locked focus.

"AuCoin, you good?" Phil would check in once he knew how much being part of something historic meant to Chris, how he quietly intervened when someone fell behind, or remained stoic as chaos swirled around them.

"Yes, Commander. All good here, sir." Chris had a smile that broke through his entire face. Phil often marveled at the young Marine's efficient hopefulness. He was a thinker, *and* a doer—a particularly useful marriage of formidable battlefield talents.

They were lucky on the days when the wind blew grit and sand off the landmines and made them visible enough to avoid. Combat engineers worked to cut paths through the fields to move forward toward the enemy and prepare defensive positions. The aftermath of a recent incident involving friendly fire was etched into every Marine's face, that bold disquiet of looming disaster in the oily sheen of the misty fog. They marched on, many blocking out distinct memories of dismemberment and death, body bags misshapen with the scorched and separated remains of their bunkmates and friends. Their family pictures forever tucked into torn pockets, their corners frayed by cramped fingers that had held on too tightly.

Phil wasn't clear where Chris was that day, or if he'd personally carried his mates away, only that he was never disheveled from lack of sleep or distracted by trepidation. Chris moved with purpose and clarity, seemingly unbothered by pressure, the ferocious heat, violent captures and uprisings of Iraqi prisoners, and the constant cacophony of alarms.

"Up, up, up!" Phil hollered to alert the men of a helicopter moving their way. The unit was pressing deeper into Kuwait, moving during the day to new positions, and digging holes into the greasy ground where they could hide and ride out enemy artillery.

The helicopter landed, but shrill orders pierced the rhythmic thud of the rotor blades.

"Gear up!" Phil instructed once he heard the warning of possible chemicals or biological substances in the air. Every Marine carried Mission Oriented Protective Posture gear that, in theory, protected them from poison designed to incapacitate or kill them. Chris may have been built like a power lifter, but he was fast and meticulous in deploying not only his MOPP 4 gear, but ensuring the other guys were buttoned up into theirs.

They stayed in that gear as temperatures pushed 114 degrees, blinking through streams of sweat beneath the gas mask, gasping for air they prayed was clean—yet always watching for signs it wasn't. It was a crap shoot they all accepted.

Whenever Phil had access to clean water, he made sure they washed their hands. Contamination wasn't just the gas that could pour through a faulty mask, it was spent shells on the ground, stepping through the decay of explosive matter and cluster bombs, the mire of minefields stuck to boots and gloves. All of it, assembled around weary arms and legs, repeatedly, whenever the dreadful warning tone sounded.

"Gear on!"

"Gear on!"

"GEAR ON!"

Phil watched eighteen and nineteen-year-olds, who had barely filled out enough to resemble a grown man, crack. He saw husbands and fathers adopt a stern expression when their first thought was breathing in gas that would scorch their lungs and put them down. What that meant to them now that a family would be left behind. What it would mean to their parents, their siblings, their nation. If they died out there, burned alive from the inside out, what would it mean to anyone?

In that peril, Chris AuCoin seemed to thrive. Phil looked around for Chris, needing him for a job or task, and often located him near a group of downtrodden and exhausted men—doing his best to make them smile. That time he found Chris deep in a hole, on his back in a makeshift bench press stance, throwing up buckets on either side of a long broom stick to maintain his strength. Chris corrected someone's wrong with grace, "*Hey, man try it this way next time, but good thinking,*" worked comfortably on his own but could be seamlessly dropped into any group in a supporting role. "*Hey, guys, tell me what you need.*"

In the military, and certainly during wartime, a unit needed to work as a cohesive whole, there was no room for individuality or self-concern. Chris embraced that like a personal mantra: Be the rock, the solid go-to, the immovable force that would never break. He wanted to take everything Kuwait threw at him and become a stronger man for it.

"Gear on!"

Ammo dumps hit with potential release of sarin gas imminent. Alarms blared in the early hours of morning. The pitch blackness of night. Awakened with bleary eyes and only seconds to assemble protective gear, they hoped for the best. *Will it even work?* They didn't know. Only that the cumbersome gear was the best chance they had.

"False alarm, boys. I think we're clear."

Were they, though?

"Gear on!"

"GEAR ON!"

It went that way for months. The Manchester Bravo Company Cold Weather Mountain Unit baked in triple digit heat while being strangled by oil contaminated air, left to guess if their government issued protective gear was functioning in a bioweapon attack, transported Iraqi soldiers trained to maim and kill, and slept only in blocks of minutes.

"Gear on!"

Like muscle memory, the blaring chemical alarms imprinted their ghastly melody on them like an unsought tattoo—until their brains developed an almost addiction to a numb preparedness. Find the one way to win. If you could.

Mask on.

Shoot whatever's in front of you.

Fight.

Survive.

As far as Brent and Paula knew, Chris was moving prisoners. That's all. No dramatics, he was doing just fine. But more than that, he needed to know they were, too. Every letter that Chris sent home to his family in New Hampshire was signed the same.

Love from your son and brother. I'm okay, if you're okay.

For many weeks, Chris took a small recording device along with him, determined to fill a tape with the goings on in the desert and eventually send it home to his parents and brothers. He thought it might be nice for them to hear his voice. On January 6th, 1991, at 11:16 am, Chris pressed record, and told his parents not of a mundane day, but of a show going in the sky.

Just passed a big old Marine on my left who's laughing at me. Listen to this! Distinct fighter jet roaring. *That's a fighter aircraft, one of twenty flown over here this morning, flying low to give the Iraqis an idea of what we're going to do to them. It's enough to pop your eardrums.*

Chris's voice, later that same afternoon.

Yesterday, we went on a little hike to the Persian Gulf. I got my feet and hands in the water of the Persian Gulf. Always hearing about that region of the world, now getting to see it. Told you about the jets flying over this morning, showing us what they can do. Pretty wild stuff. Going to church around three this afternoon. See you on the other side.

He told them of an article he'd read in the *Stars and Stripes* military newspaper, alleging there was some US troop grumbling going on. Chris wanted his parents to know a different version.

From what I've seen, it's not exactly home, but it's not hell. All that complaining you're seeing on TV, take it with a grain of salt. Bunch of wimps complaining, hopefully we'll show them how it's done.

By January 18th, Chris was familiar with the commonly ordered defensive position, deep in a fighting hole he'd dug. He was more honest then, as he explained his role and what was happening around him.

Sitting in my fox hole up to my neck in depth. Protecting a base camp. There's a base camp in our rear, we're guarding it. Which is part of my job. I'm sure you've heard on the 17th, which is the 16th for you. At oh-one our time, the US went into Iraq and bombed the shit out of—excuse me, pardon my French—bombed the heck out of it. I believe that process will be going on for some time. We're along the perimeter so I assume there's no way they're going to get anywhere near us, going to get waxed.

Chris also hinted at the weariness he was feeling.

Little tired today, can hear it in my voice. We don't sleep much here, nap every now and again, but very much still on the alert. Just to be safe, we don't sleep at night, maintain alertness. Night vision goggles allow us to see; it gets pretty dark here.

Measured, a hint of the truth, but only as much as Chris preferred to divulge. He figured his parents back home were voraciously watching TV and listening for radio updates on the war. He wanted them to know he was always good. He was okay.

I'm following everyone's advice who's been in this situation before. Keep your chin up and your butt down. If any freak thing did happen, I'm right down here with no problems as far as cover.

As Chris went on to speak into the recorder from that defensive position, he had a final message for whoever would one day listen to his words.

We hear a rumble every now and again. Everything is pretty much kosher. Taking my recorder out of my case and seeing I'm just about out of tape.

That was the final recording Chris made from his fox hole during Operation Desert Storm. Throughout the tape, he reminds his parents to watch for his letters and not worry too much, because the news didn't always reflect what was going on from his position and perspective. His protective stance wrapped not only around his men over there, but his family back home. He never once told them anything he knew they couldn't handle. He didn't discuss what he'd been through. Chris was endlessly and deliberately okay.

Chris, Buddy Hackett, Kevin Sullivan, and Phil Smith, all made it home to New Hampshire. The lucky ones, as they knew they were, but still forever changed by what they'd seen, heard, and done. An internal residue had been planted, one that would interfere with their bodies and minds, and it was as thick as any oil fire in Kuwait.

CHAPTER SEVEN
YELLOW RIBBONS FOR CHRISTMAS

A national sentiment was sweeping across small towns and big cities in late 1990 and into 1991. Troops who, decades before, had been publicly shunned after returning from foreign conflict were instead celebrated and prayed for. The Gulf War that began that summer and, for most intents, wrapped mere months later as the calendar ticked over to a new year, had spawned an ideological unity. A sentient belief that America had built the finest fighting force in the world, and her citizens were proud of the military supremacy displayed overseas. Americans gathered with cheer. Children sat on their father's shoulders, clapping along to songs they learned in grade school—their lyrics full of words like honor, freedom, and an earned right to be known as the best country on earth.

Merrimack, New Hampshire was also celebrating the holiday season. It was December, and the AuCoins had the chance to visit with Chris prior to his deployment with the Marine reserve unit while he was training in North Carolina. Not everyone in their town knew Chris AuCoin would be on a plane to the Middle East as soon as New Year's Eve, but once they did, admiration and support for his family followed. Townspeople who had seen reports from elsewhere—those other places that had sent a young soldier to war only to have him separated from his flock forever kept Chris and the AuCoins close to their hearts.

Beep, beep!

Brent punched the horn in the middle of the steering wheel and waved a hand outside of the open driver's side window. The heat inside the cab cranked on high, humming out a stream of warmth that kept the windshield clear. In his dad's truck, Brent rode the brakes to carefully pull out of the staging area of a shopping plaza. Positioned behind one of the marching bands and groupings of twirlers in sparkly uniforms spinning batons with long red and green streamers cascading off each end, Brent kept his place in the parade procession as it turned down Old Route Three. He kept one eye on Paula's whereabouts on the pavement next to the truck's wheels, and the other on his two boys in the bed of the truck, already on a sugar high from ingesting fists full of the candy they were supposed to toss out to the crowd.

The AuCoin family's vision for the float they'd decorated for that year's Christmas parade reflected the service of the son who couldn't be there with them, and the many others overseas. Brent built a giant wooden A-frame structure to hold a seven-foot balsam in the bed of the truck, securing it with twine and wires. They wrapped its branches with hundreds of small yellow ribbons Paula, Nate, and Chad tied themselves. Lagana's Deli donated rolls of deli paper Paula then used to make posters colored in red, white, and blue in honor of the troops. She gathered other promotional billboards from all the local recruiter offices, so each branch of the military was represented. The truck was transformed into a rolling symbol of patriotism complete with speakers that blared out Lee Greenwood's anthem, *Proud to Be an American.*

Nate and Chad felt Chris's absence during that parade. Young as they were, they prayed for their brother's safe return home and sensed the gravity of what war meant—on a granular level—to their mom and dad who'd clutched each other's hands as they'd watched Chris leave home to serve. They imagined how glorious the following Christmas would be, when Chris was home and their family was whole once again.

"Man, don't give away all the Tootsie Rolls!" Nate admonished Chad, who was elbow deep in the bucket of candy between their knees.

"I'm not, but what if I did?" Chad smirked back. "Whatcha gonna do about it?"

Nate pushed his little brother's shoulder but kept quiet. Neither son wanted to aggravate Paula, who had an uncanny knack for hearing and seeing everything they did.

"Just don't, okay?"

"Ugh, fine."

They recognized classmates and friends in the rows of people assembled on the sidewalks. Their parents also recognized the reporter from the local TV station approaching the truck with a man holding a cumbersome camera on his shoulder right behind her. Jennifer Crompton was working her way to eventual roles as evening anchor and eventual News Director of WMUR-TV. That day, she was assigned to cover the Merrimack Christmas parade, and learned a young Marine named Chris AuCoin was among the local Marine Reserve unit headed to Saudi Arabia in support of Operation Desert Storm. She approached the truck with her microphone and introduced herself to Brent as he slowed to a stop on the route. He later appeared on the station's evening newscasts, echoing his family's and town's pride in their country and holiday tradition. As she put her report together, Jennifer was struck by the support, then and now.

"Weekend reporting was filled with interviews with families, neighbors, veterans, and local leaders expressing so much pride, hope, and concern. The parents of Chris AuCoin were among them. Whether in their words or in the heartfelt wishes written on their faces, expressing a common denominator among loved ones, that their son would return home, alive, leaving the scars of war behind. The reality, even these many years since, would prove that to be gut-wrenchingly impossible for him, and far too many others."

Decades later, that day remained in her memory. As it did for Brent and Paula. They, too, would never forget the parade and the massive turnout. The warm hugs and supportive sentiments shared by friends and strangers. The boys' fingers cramping at night, exhausted from manipulating tiny strips of yellow ribbons into enough bows to fill every branch on that tree in the bed of their grandfather's truck. They were chatty when they arrived back home and cleaned up, humming Christmas carols, eager for Paula's milky hot chocolate and maybe a Christmas movie on TV that night. They shared the Tootsie Rolls Chad kept for them as the candy bucket emptied out. A mother's heart held a unique talent—to swell simply by what her eyes could see, and during that parade, it was the pride Paula felt for her sons, and a military mission she and Brent were compelled to support. They believed it was righteous and proper, that Chris was doing important work and he and every allied soldier would be protected by an almighty hand. It was a position of faith the AuCoins vigorously defended, even when the pushback felt harsh and personal.

—★—

Paula's father, gone before she'd fully grown up, had previously left Leona to serve in World War II. She'd felt his absence during that time as deep as any worried wife can, but it scarred her. It was a combination of her husband's physical absence and a fear of his work, though not in a combat role, that thrust Leona into a panic during Chris's deployment. Awash with that renewed dread and hollow agitation of a worst-case scenario, Leona was reduced to wracking sobs, her hands in a death grip on her coffee mug in Paula's kitchen, as tears of anguish poured out of her like a geyser. Drip, drip, dripping on the tablecloth. Paula counted eight quarter-sized wet gray circles.

"Mom, Chris is okay. I have faith he will be fine."

"But, Paula…"

"Mom. Mom, come on now.

"I wish I could say that, too. But, sweetie, is he? How do we know? How do we know what's happening there right now?"

"Mom, please."

"But, but…"

"MOM!"

Leona's leaky eyes went wide. She bit back the dramatic cascade she couldn't help but heap upon her already stressed daughter—and offered a half apology,

"I worry because I love Chris so very much. I can't imagine something happening to our Chris!"

Paula squeezed the bridge of her nose and regulated her breathing. Lord knew she'd managed Leona's impassioned eccentricity well enough through the years, but she was struggling herself. Didn't her mom see that? Missing Chris and worrying about him on a desert battlefield was exhausting her, yet life went on and her family needed her to be present and competent, as she always was. Leona had to chill, and Paula told her as much.

"Mom, I hear you, and we all love Chris. But you really need to knock it off."

They hugged goodbye and agreed that Leona couldn't help how much she loved Chris, but would try to stop it from making her unhinged and hysterical.

Brent listened from the living room, his foot crossed over his knee, bobbing out the nervous excess of energy he couldn't expend. It lived in him every day at work, spinning like hot bile through his gut, infiltrating every thought. He'd come home at night, keep up an appropriate stream of dinner table conversation, and then immediately take up a position in the living room: In his chair, glued to the TV. He sat there unmoved into the earliest hours of the next day, analyzing the CNN correspondents' reports, hanging on every mention of scud missile strikes, targeted locations, and… one February night… word of an attack on an American forces' barracks.

"How would we know if that's Chris?" Paula whispered, her voice twisted by anguish for days.

"I don't know." It was the raw truth of their predicament. A forlornness shared across every American state, every military family in towns near and far. Soldiers had been killed. But was it *their* soldier?

Was it Chris?

"Brent, come to bed. It's late." Paula would coax Brent from the 24-hour war coverage, return the living room to its darkened middle-of-the-night setting, and then feel his restlessness—that unspent energy—toss and turn him around for many more hours. She slept fitfully herself. Anxiously stared at the phone. Would word come via a ring, or a knock on the door?

Was it Chris?

While over two dozen American souls were lost in that attack, Chris's wasn't among them. The AuCoins prayed for the soldiers and their families and wept relieved tears for their own. As they tend to with large scale military loss and conflict, opinions emerged, and difficult conversations were had. Sometimes, they happened close to home and with the ones the AuCoins loved the most. Leona wasn't the only grandparent having conflicted thoughts.

—★—

"By God, we have no business even being there. Our government sends our Chris, all these young men and women over there? For what?"

"Dad," Brent began, keeping his reply calm and measured even though he was broiling with anger. He would one day realize how hypersensitive he'd become during Chris's deployment, but that call with the father he adored felt enormously disruptive to his entire posture. Brent's routine had become predictable—he'd consume the news and government position wholly as a salve he applied upon himself to endure the unprecedented desperation he felt every day knowing Chris was fighting a war. Brent had to believe in his heart that American Forces were in it for the right reasons! And he did. He always would. Fractures were inadmissible in remaining galvanized as a father and head of his family. Chris needed him to hold the line at home.

"No, wait a minute, Brent. Listen to me. You need to realize the government does not have their best inter—"

"Dad! I won't have this conversation with you! I can't. I believe in this. I have to. For me, and for Chris!"

It may have been the sharpest exchange ever to happen between father and son, and the taste of it remained in Brent's mouth for a very long time.

Well into 1991, Chris returned home. The family tension melted into relief. But to say no time was wasted getting right back to work would be understating Chris's determination to climb from the back of one galloping horse and immediately put his foot into the stirrup of another.

CHAPTER EIGHT
SOMETHING HAPPENED HERE

All those late nights on patrol in Saudi Arabia and Kuwait, discussing his future with Buddy and others, had winnowed into a more specific and clearer path for Chris. He'd achieved his dream of becoming a Marine. Now, he wanted to be a cop. Better yet, he wanted to be a great cop. It started with a call to the Chief of Police in Amherst, New Hampshire, a town east of Merrimack and similar in size and makeup. Chris was offered a job when he returned home to New Hampshire, enrolled in the mandatory training program at the New Hampshire Police Standards and Training Council in Concord, easily breezed through it, and began his first job as a police officer.

"Where's your head at?" Brent asked one day over morning coffee. He was still traveling quite a bit, but wanted to be available to Chris if he needed to shed any disturbing sentiments from his deployment, or more thoroughly talk out his plans with the Amherst PD. "You feeling good?"

Chris's face split into that grin. He came home looking the same, yet Brent knew he was a different young man inside, as everyone was who'd seen war up close. He declined to debrief either Brent or Paula on the full load of his months overseas, and never would, and by their standards of knowing him better than anyone, Chris was his typical upbeat, energetic, physically imposing self. Strong, earnest, and steady. Their rock had come back with nary a chip missing.

Or so it seemed.

"I'm great, Dad. Couldn't be better."

Brent had constructed a mass of unasked questions in his head, and they knocked against each other like ice cubes as he watched his son sit before him, clad in a new blue police uniform. *Tell me, Chris. Tell me your burdens, release them to me. Are you okay?*

He held back the urge to pester or poke, making a burbling sound instead that indicated an understanding. Chris said he's great. Maybe he was. Brent's crossed leg jiggled against the leg of the table, in that familiar way he'd adopted to let an inanimate object absorb the fussy yip he held in his throat. He'd continued to watch newscasts and listen to reports of soldiers returning from war physically unharmed, but still… somewhat off. Changed. Chris showed no obvious signs of that, but Brent wasn't sure what he was looking for either.

He watched his son chew around a mouthful of oatmeal, his hand steady on the spoon, eyes clear, forehead relaxed and smooth. Chris was fine, wasn't he? This young man who'd fought for his country before he was legally able to buy himself a beer at the bar down the road. Was this odd feeling Brent had merely a case of secondhand reflection? Hearing of something and then making it personal? Either way, Brent wanted Chris to listen. To reinforce the obvious. Put it right there on the front of his mind as he left their house that morning and began another dangerous job in law enforcement.

"Hey, Chris?"

"Ya?" He looked up, eyebrows bobbing in preparation to receive.

"Son, you know I'm always here, right? Even if I'm away you can always talk to me and Mom. We just want to make sure you know we're here if you need us. Being a cop is a tough job."

Chris bent himself intently over his bowl and did Brent a favor by thinking about what he'd just said rather than tossing out a fast response.

He studied his father's point. Let it marinate over him rather than wash away—even though Chris always thought of himself as invincible.

"I know that, Dad. I will come to you if I need to. Promise."

The conversation would surface as a tiny glitch at the back of Brent's head through the years, mixed in with those hard examinations of time, events, and the wishes that had gone ungranted. The hardness of Chris's chosen career would make itself painfully obvious from the earliest days on the job. Brent heard bits and pieces of awful police incidents unfold with Chris in a pivotal role and yet would wait out all the years he had left in this world for the talks that never happened. Chris wouldn't come to his parents in that way because he wasn't built to. He encountered an incident, dealt with it, trained harder to rise through the ranks, and moved on. But what he saw and did in his work was buried inside, in a secret place Chris never let anyone enter.

—★—

"Child involved. Proceed with caution. Child on scene."

In his early weeks with the Amherst Police Department, dispatch called Chris to an incident. He acknowledged the communication while in his cruiser, confirmed receipt of information, and proceeded to the address he was given. It was one of the first calls of his career, and Chris felt his pulse quicken. He ran the dispatcher's relay through his mind.

An address. A child. Something bad had just occurred.

Chris turned the corner onto the street. It was lit by late afternoon daylight, around the time children would be stepping off buses as they were delivered home from school.

Child involved.

The worst cases always contained those two words.

A child had just walked down the stairs of his bus, turned the handle on his front door, and stepped into a nightmare.

Chris exited his cruiser and immediately discovered the young boy on the front steps of his house. His mind ticked through the training still fresh in his mind. He followed procedure. The Marines had protocols, so did police officers. Some were the same, while others drastically different. He rapidly checked off the next steps in his new role of responding officer: Assess the entirety of what was going on. Was this boy in danger? Was there an active threat to the kid, to Chris? Were there suspects here, who were they, where were they hiding? Witnesses? Find them. He was the first officer on scene and would be responsible for all investigative efforts that followed, along with completing the incident report. Within seconds, Chris scanned the house, the appearance of the child—*was he hurt, bloody?*—and approached.

Nothing stirred in the yard.

No sounds from the house.

The boy was exhibiting cues of emotional shock. Chris checked his body and found no trauma, injury, or physical impairment. No, the kid was okay. But something had happened there. That boy had seen something that would alter every day that came after. As the sun set on that Amherst home, and responding agencies took over the case, Chris knew when it rose again, the house would never get back what was lost inside. Sure, it may look the same, but any shred of innocence it once held was gone. Stolen away.

He was late getting home that night. Brent and Paula kept dinner warm in the oven and waited. When they all sat down to eat, Chris was quiet, more observant. He watched Nate and Chad quibble over the usual topics—who would eat the last of the mashed potatoes, and who had left his dirty socks on the floor. Brent and Paula exchanged concerned glances, but didn't push Chris to talk or share anything about his day.

Small towns have a way of confirming news long before any reporter can. They'd already heard of that house. That young boy. The father who had killed himself while his son was at school. What that child had discovered after he tossed his lunchbox on the couch and went looking for his dad, eager to tell him all about his day.

Chris brought up that boy to Brent, speaking of him with deliberate emotional separation. This happened. That followed. Facts only. Much like a court stenographer who listened and recorded events for history's sake. He never once infused himself into the discussion. Brent never dared ask, toeing that imaginary line he didn't want to put Chris in a position of crossing. New questions, tucked away to join all the others.

But Chris, how did you feel walking in on that?

How are you coping with what you saw?

What about you, Chris, how are you doing?

Something bad had happened that day, and Chris had seen it all.

CHAPTER NINE
REAL TIME DECISIONS

Dead of night, dull headlights splashed a fan of illumination on the parking lot of Salzburg Square, a charming shopping center in Amherst known for its unique stores, small business feel, and elegant exclusivity. The stores were locked shut, dark inside, deserted. The driver of a vehicle casing the place noted the quietness of his target. His brake lights lit red. He killed the engine and lights. Sat in the silence, gauging any new sounds. No one would be there at that hour.

He didn't anticipate the silent alarm he would trigger as he attempted to rob one store of its high-end contents.

On patrol, Chris clocked the incoming call from dispatch, and within minutes pulled into Salzburg Square. Checking his weapon, he carefully exited the cruiser and scanned the suspicious vehicle. It was empty. He'd also made sure to transmit back to the police department his location pursuant to a change in his status. He was now about to enter the woods adjacent to the shopping area, convinced he'd seen a shadow dash into the cover of tall pines.

"Unknown weapon status." He relayed back one final time. "In foot pursuit of subject."

He couldn't tell if the suspect was armed. Knew it was a possibility.

With the procedural steps taken care of, Chris dragged some air deep into his lungs to boost oxygen and stabilize his body's preparedness to escalate energy output. He maintained a steady breathing pattern as his quad muscles elongated to accommodate his quickening pace. The building was long, shaped somewhat like a crescent moon that wrapped around itself, with a distinctly jutted out corner and backside that abutted massive pine trees and thick foliage. The driver had lead time out there, but Chris could hear him crunching through underbrush as he rounded that corner into the building's exterior. The bony snap of twigs pinged to his right, somewhere in the maze of branches built like webs of scaffolding that rose into the blackness of the cloudless sky. But Chris could see exactly what he needed to do to get himself close enough to take down the suspect and squash the danger of this incident escalating into something worse.

He adjusted his position. Angling himself diagonally against the noise he'd just heard, Chris darted through the needle-like branches, ignoring them as they tore through this skin and ripped at his uniform. Wiping away the sweat so his vision stayed clear, Chris was at a slightly higher elevation and able to look down. He saw a streak of clothing. A laboring figure that still had a head start. Chris had to cut him off.

He swung his body sharply to the left, heat exploding through his boots with each step, ankles tweaking with the sharp swivel while still in rapid motion. His fists pumped. Eyes slit in concentrated determination to flush this guy out of the gloom. He zigzagged around the pitch of ground, caught himself on disturbed gravel. Stayed upright. Moved in.

The goal was uncomplicated even as branches snapped against his face. Nicks and cuts bled out tiny streams of wetness down his cheeks. His nose ran from exertion. Chris drilled down on his intent.

Get this guy. Figure out how to do that in real time. Do his job.

Chris's detour put him directly in front of a huge rock that just happened to be perfectly positioned to launch himself from. The target was still ahead, but if Chris went airborne, hung over him just right, he calculated he could grab a foot, a shoulder, some body part to take him down.

His right foot planted on the rock's side. Left foot stretched forward to lead Chris's full length through the airspace and preserve his body's position for the assault from above. Somewhere midair, Chris realized he would likely hit the target with his whole body and prepared himself for impact. The man below never saw it coming. Chris's mighty chest slammed into his spinal cord and shoulder blades with a resounding thud that must have dazzled his consciousness into a twilight state. He went down hard. Groaned a few times, stunned to realize he was flat on the ground with no memory of how he got there.

Chris cuffed the suspect's limp hands behind his back, dragged him back to his cruiser and delivered him to the department. He diligently reported the incident in full account of every moment.

The next morning, Brent had questions, and if he were to be honest with himself, several concerns, too. In that small town way, news had spread about the incident at Salzburg Square. The daring pursuit through the woods. Brent and Paula knew Chris was on duty. They noticed small lines on his face where his skin had been torn. His knuckles, somewhat swollen. Otherwise, Chris was unhurt and entirely undisturbed.

"What time was it?" Brent asked as they sat together having breakfast.

"Late."

Brent nodded, his stomach dropping. "Did you have backup, Chris?"

"They knew where I was, Dad."

Sure, Brent thought. But knowing Chris's location versus being next right to him was very different. "I meant was someone there with you? Were you alone? Is that protocol?" His breath strained as Brent felt it going wild. "Chris, come on now. That seems a bit dangerous."

Chris's expression didn't lodge displeasure as much as perplexity. While he understood his dad would have questions, he registered them as interesting—that his on-the-job technique would be debated. Misinterpreted as something other than securing a perp through intelligent and aggressive judgement.

"Not sure what you're getting at, Dad, but I did what I needed to do to bring that guy in. I'd do it again."

It was not disrespectful, nor impolite, but there was a finality in Chris's tone.

Brent rolled that around in his mind. His son's declaration caused him even more displeasure. It felt reckless to him. Crude, even, with the potential to seriously injure Chris and the suspect. The room got quiet. Father and son each drawing further into themselves.

"You could have hurt yourself," Brent went on to say. A completion of the conversation that allowed him to get another point in. One that Chris needed. "You're not unbreakable."

To that, Chris grinned at his dad. That big smile that split his face until his eyes crinkled.

"I'm not? Are you sure about that, Dad?"

—★—

To look only at his exterior, someone might say Chris was very close to impenetrable, but no one knew him on the inside like his parents. His heart was tender, and when Chris came home one night around Christmastime that year, Brent and Paula noticed he was troubled. Not from another wild chase through the woods, or a messy crime scene, but instead from what that season meant to him: Family, joy, the anticipation a child felt knowing Santa was about to land on his roof and deliver new hockey skates, a video game, and maybe a puppy.

Two parents in town had just been arrested for stealing items from local stores and turning them around to sell to someone else. With that cash, they declined to buy Christmas gifts for their three sons. No, they paid out the bundle for drugs.

All Chris could think about during their arrest were three little boys who would wake up in foster care that Christmas morning, wondering where their parents had gone, and why Santa never got their wish lists that year.

Three little boys, not so different from him, Nate, and Chad—but worlds apart only because, unlike the AuCoin boys, they'd been born to a family ill-prepared to care for them.

The randomness of it all crushed him.

CHAPTER TEN
ASCENSION

Life also worked that way to deliver people to Chris who would build the connective tissue of the rest of his life.

"Mom, Dad, I've met someone."

Brent and Paula met Tracy shortly after she and Chris had started dating, and around the time they moved out of Merrimack and back to Brent's hometown of Jaffrey. Tracy was working dispatch for the Amherst Police Department while she finished her nursing degree at the University of New Hampshire. Well positioned to understand the demands of a cop's wife, Tracy's voice had often been the calm instructive one back at the station directing Chris to his next call. The trust between them had started there, and quickly bloomed into more.

"Chris was very sweet," Tracy reflected. "A gentle, big guy. He asked the sergeant for permission to ask me out."

Chris and Tracy married in 1993. By the next year, their first of three daughters was on the way. Chris was just twenty-three, Tracy three years older. The fact their son was to be a young father was something Brent and Paula could relate to. They knew he'd be loving, caring, and strong for his family.

"Let's head down to the beach for a bit, leave the girls here to catch up." Brent threw an arm around Chris's shoulders and led him to the back door. Their new house in Jaffrey was more of an old cottage, with two dwellings on the property that sat near Contoocook Lake. Brent and Paula lived in one cottage while they renovated the other, eventually moving into the larger home with peaceful views of twinkling sunlight as it danced on the water. Visits to his parents' new house were a welcomed distraction for Chris, as both he and Tracy kept their busy work schedule and got ready for their new baby. The AuCoins were blissfully awaiting the arrival of their first grandchild and doted on Tracy whenever she came by. After three boys, Paula felt a natural maternal pull toward a young woman who'd entered her family and was about to bring along even more members.

"Tracy, tell me about work. How are you feeling? Are you getting enough rest?" Paula cupped Tracy's elbow with a tender touch. "Let me get you some water." She marveled at Tracy's growing stomach, imagining the child—Chris's child—developing inside. She wanted Tracy to always feel comfortable and welcomed at their home.

"Off you go, you two. We'll be fine back here." She waved to Brent and Chris. "See you in a bit."

Brent and Chris took off toward the pond, walking together down the narrow street that brought them to the shore. "How's work?" Brent started. They spoke with Chris regularly now that he'd moved out on his own with his new wife, and they back to Jaffrey, but there was a tactile exquisiteness in being able to see and feel him in person. To touch his shoulder, absorb his heartbeat in their embrace. Brent relished that togetherness.

"Good." Chris cocked his head in thought. Paused. "You know, Dad, I'd say it's really good. I'm getting a lot of experience. It's different from Amherst. More gritty work, and a lot of process and procedure. I'm figuring it out, though. I feel like I'm finding my place."

They wound down the dirt path to the shore and looked out over the water, its surface shimmering in the golden light like the 4th of July sparklers the boys used to hold like torches as they dashed through the moonlight that hung over their back yard. Brent took some time to come around to Chris's goals in law enforcement. Similarly to why they'd tried to intervene when he was determined to become a Marine, he and Paula were proud yet concerned. Worried about Chris in such a dangerous and stressful profession. They also knew he was chasing the big dream: to become a New Hampshire state trooper. That year, he'd earned his way in. Amherst had been just a temporary starting point, and no one who knew Chris's determined demeanor doubted he would pass the sixteen-week course to become a state trooper. He'd crushed it with distinction. Chris was already on the radar within the command structure as someone to watch.

Brent picked up a rock with a smooth edge, the perfect form for skipping. He angled his arm and held the rock between his thumb and pointer finger.

"Four." Chris predicted.

"Come on, really? Four? That's lame."

"Nope. I say four."

"Okay, here goes."

Brent launched the rock in a nuanced release to help it find just enough air to keep it climbing back up even after skimming the water. The rock touched down. Rose again. They counted one, two, three…

"Six, Dad. Nice!"

Six skips.

"You underestimated me, son."

"You'd think by now I'd know better than to do that. Sorry, Pop."

Brent was the champ of rock skipping, but the boys were quite proficient, too. Paula, even, had considerable skill with a nice, flat rock. A fun, competitive escape they often enjoyed during camping adventures, trips to the beach, and here, at the lake behind the AuCoin's new house.

Wind whipped across the water, inspiring those nicknamed ripples to form towards the middle.

"Cat's paws," Chris pointed out. "See 'em, right there?"

"Sure do." But Brent's eyes were on his son who was about to join the most exclusive men's club ever known. At times, it took his breath away, the pureness of fatherhood—banal in commonplace and yet impeccably ethereal. Chris was about to enter that transcendent realm and yet as he examined every feature on his face, Brent could still see the little boy he'd once been. He swallowed. Steadied his voice to speak.

"Just keep doing what you're doing, Chris. Keep your head about you and follow procedure. Especially now, make a good name for yourself in the ranks."

"That's the plan."

"How about we head back, see what the girls are up to."

Brent kept the conversation light on the walk back to the house, but he ruminated on many unspoken topics. Chris had a lot of his father in him, that driving urge to be successful mixed with the need to be more, do more, produce more than everyone else. Brent considered it a low confidence bar in himself, and while he never could brand that onto Chris—nor would he want to define him like that—he saw a relentlessness in him that mirrored his own. It was ambition, yet somehow supercharged. The source of that, in Chris though, may be something Brent would never know. He could, however, impart some ways to work around it.

"Make sure you talk to Tracy, Chris. When you come home after work. Talk to your wife, include her in your day. I didn't do that for Mom, and I should have. I really should have made her part of my work, but instead I shielded her from it. Don't keep everything locked up inside you."

Chris nodded. "We talk, Dad. Tracy more than anyone knows this job. Our life together is very much built on that."

"Okay."

But Brent was still wrestling with complicated thoughts on that walk. Thoughts that tasted like vinegar in his mouth. The life Chris had chosen, what he would encounter in the act of doing his job—the dirty underbelly of society where criminals lurked. Drugs, disrespect for the police, guns, abuse, and violence. All the things he'd tried to protect his family from were now the daily threats of his son's career. If Chris was like him in any way, Brent worried he would toil in that impossible place of insufficiency, forcing himself to an unsustainable amplitude. Be more. Do more. Produce more. Now, he was about to become a father, which changed the game entirely, like pressing the HIGH button on a man's internal pressure cooker.

Brent wanted to say more, but a noise stirred the air that otherwise was still, save for the sounds of nature.

"Hear that?" he asked Chris.

"Ya."

They followed what, at first, was a low hum a few hundred yards away near the public beach area of the lake. "What's he doing here?" Brent wondered. The driver of a late model rusted out car was speeding through the entryway beach markers and kicking up the sand. "He can't do that."

"No." Chris stated. "He can't. I'm going to check it out."

"Chris, wait." But Chris was already on his way.

Pumping the gas pedal to churn through the sand, the driver had gotten the car stuck and his tires went flat. The engine revved and tires spun; he couldn't dig himself out. Brent followed Chris as he approached the car, noted the position of the driver and three other passengers now out of the vehicle, and flanked around the tires. They pushed it free and climbed back in.

"Hey!" Chris yelled, keeping a hand near his belt and hurrying his steps closer to the car. "Hey, stop! You guys can't be doing that here. Hey, hey! Hold on a second!"

"Chris, let's just leave them alone. Let's go."

But Chris saw a wrong. Brent sensed he would take control of this situation and make sure there was no harm done to the beach or anyone walking down the woodsy road this car had been traveling on. These guys, this car, were potential threats.

If they heard him, they defiantly ignored Chris's command to stop. Instead, the jalopy with flat tires caught some solid road and accelerated straight at Brent and Chris.

"Hey!" Chris screamed at them. "Stop. I said stop!"

Brent's breath quickened. Chris was trained, but he was still his son. His child! When the four occupants braked with a jolt, they quickly exited the car and threw down an aggressive confrontation.

"Yo, man, back up. We're packin'." One of them, the driver, motioned toward his own waist, which Brent took as a threat that he was armed. Four men, potentially locked and loaded, kept moving towards Chris—whose empty fingers were twitching; he never carried his service revolver when he was off duty. Brent's reaction was primal. He had one job: He had to protect Chris and bring this to an end. As the foursome separated to show how outmatched he and Chris were, Brent pounced. He ran toward the car, threw an arm around the neck of the guy who claimed he had a gun, and landed with a thud on its hood. He felt resistance, but hoisted himself over the thrashing limbs, aware of the screaming around him, and Chris's instructions for everyone to stop and get away from the car. It felt like an hour but was probably more like a minute or two before Brent realized the guy beneath him had gone limp. He stopped struggling.

"All right, all right, man, get off me. Get off!"

By then, Chris was corralling the group closer, into a tighter clump, to maintain control.

"Stop!" he demanded. Brent engaged in one last skirmish with the driver, then—as if the fog of violence had lifted—he could hear Chris yelling to get back. He leaned over, hands on his knees to gulp in air.

"What on earth," he muttered. Chris's eyes were wide, his stance firm, positioned toward the four men as sirens blared.

"Chris, are you okay?" Brent noticed his son's nose. It was bloody and bent. His head turned to the loud crackle of new sound and blue lights traveling rapidly down the road toward them. The police were almost there. He had no idea who'd called them in. He was still trying to figure out what had just happened!

The incident ended with four young men hauled off in two cruisers, as Chris and Brent took a drive down to the Jaffrey Police Department for a debrief, and later to the hospital in nearby Peterborough for cuts, bruises, and to confirm via blood test they hadn't been exposed to HIV.

"They also had to attend to Chris's broken nose," Tracy told Paula. "One of the guys head butted him." Tracy had been the one to call the police for help.

The dinner with Chris and Tracy, ruined, and the insanity of that experience haunted Brent for some time. Troubled by the whiplash of its postmortem, Brent analyzed the incident moment-by-moment. Had Chris intervened when he shouldn't have? Was it proper procedure to? If they'd walked back to the house would that car have careened into an innocent family taking a walk before dinner? Did any of them really have a gun? Would a more seasoned police officer have handled it differently? Did Brent bear responsibility? Did he make it harder for Chris?

Hours passed. His mind whirled. Eventually, Brent did something that night that he'd failed to do during most of his successful career—he talked at length with Paula about what had happened near the beach. He told her every bit of it, the dizzying tension and breakneck intensification, the physical position he took and single-minded focus on protecting Chris. Their son, hurt. The police, responding to Tracy's concern when they didn't come home, lights on and siren blaring, pulling in to take over. His and Chris's official relay to the officers at the station of what had transpired. While Chris had left his parents that night very much the same, Brent had been changed. He had seen police work up close, and it was terrifying.

Chris mentioned the incident to Tracy, but in ways and words they both were used to. *Suspects contained. Stupid whack jobs just messin' around.* Because to them, it was all part of the job. A job Chris was fast-tracking, elevating to heights even his parents never imagined, and earning a reputation as one of the finest ever to come through the New Hampshire State Police.

When baby Kelsey arrived, Chris had already bought his first house in Merrimack, was saving up to buy another, and pursuing big opportunities at work whenever they opened. By the time he and Tracy welcomed two more daughters, Chris had hopped around to troop stations across the state, earned promotions in rank, and was constructing a reputation as one of the premiere law enforcement figures in New Hampshire. No one was surprised when Chris was tapped to try out for the NHSP SWAT team. As it was with the USMC, he seemed to have been built for the role. The pace of Chris's ascension was almost unmatched.

Brent worked on himself during that time to find a measure of peace with Chris's career. Rounded out the learning curve of being the father of a man who served and protected. While that weird car incident at the beach still bothered him, he learned to trust Chris as much as he put his trust in God's protection—yet never elevating Chris above the Lord who Brent believed kept him safe.

Chris had built himself into a physical and mental behemoth, both disciplined and exact. Paula adopted the mindset of not worrying until there was something to worry about. It kept her grounded in the moment even when her mind tried to whip up all sorts of terrifying scenarios starring Chris and the NHSP.

And there was always that small town chatter to contend with. When something was going down, the AuCoins were among the first to know about it—and that Chris was probably right in the middle of it.

CHAPTER 11
COLEBROOK

The northern town of Colebrook, New Hampshire, was known for moose sightings and casual gatherings of neighbors who preferred space, independence, and living out in nature. In August of 1997, tiny Colebrook was shaken to its core by deadly violence. The sort of shock no one in the town could imagine—until bullets were flying and well-known, beloved community members were lost to deranged rage and gunfire. State trooper Chris AuCoin was on duty for Troop B and the radio communication coming in was outrageous.

Shots fired! Shots fired! IGA Supermarket parking lot. Troopers down. Troopers down.

The gunman had a history, police knew who he was: hostile, full of a perceived personal vengeance held against his family. A widower, and gun owner. He fought with the town often, its people occasionally and had scores to settle. When a state trooper radioed another trooper of his location and exited his cruiser to approach a run-down pickup truck in the IGA supermarket parking lot, the firing of an assault rifle cracked through the air—the unmistakable yet incongruous sound in an otherwise idyllically peaceful place. When the sun set on that summer day—the blue bird Chamber of Commerce type of seasonal perfection day—four people were dead, including two troopers.

Chris started his career with the New Hampshire state police in Troop B, which ran through Hillsborough County, and included two of the state's largest cities, Manchester and Nashua, along the southern tier. Colebrook was a three hour drive due north, which was too far for immediate response to the shooting, but Chris was called in to provide support. Paula knew that long before it had been officially confirmed. She'd been perusing the aisles at the Hallmark store in town when the radio squawked out a breaking news report.

SWAT team called to an incident up north. Troopers down.

She threw the items she'd been carrying back onto a shelf and raced out to the parking lot. Chris and Tracy had moved to a house in Rindge, New Hampshire to save money for a bigger home. Paula pulled into the driveway and raced to their front door.

"Tracy, something's going on!" she blurted as her daughter-in-law opened the door. "Where's Chris? Have you heard from Chris?"

While the horror of Colebrook was difficult and jarring for the entire law enforcement community, Chris realized many things about himself during the exceptionally violent incident New Hampshire would never forget. While he was still at the beginning of his career, he did the job with exceptional calm and decorum. He expected a lot from himself and followed a rigid daily practice that revolved around fitness, and developing a distinct ability to commit entirely to an incident as a team member. That was different from the smoldering oil fields of Kuwait, where Chris made it his job to protect the entire lot of soldiers. This was taking those custodial skills and advancing them into a larger brand of selflessness and sub-calmness that few can attain. Somehow, Chris found in himself a mental dexterity to reprogram his brain in moments of extreme stress and uncertainty. When chaos disrupted the physiological process and fused focus into a tight tunnel devoid of auditory disruptions, or in police instances, blocked out commands or orders, Chris displayed the opposite.

His zone became larger, more compatible with a whole environmental tactical awareness only the most successful operators worked within. He had the sort of mental flexibility that matched his physical strength. That, combined with Chris's all-in attitude put him in line for the state's most highly trained team of troopers: SWAT.

Once selected, Chris had to train harder than ever to stay on the team. He became a specialist in weapons and the breaching equipment SWAT used for dynamic entries meant to stun and disrupt but not always kill. The goal of any SWAT mission was to mitigate the threat but protect all life. To Chris, that meant everything, and he approached the job with an open mind for how he, personally, might be able to make it even safer for himself and everyone around him.

Like Chris, Kevin Duffy had a military background. A one-time Army captain, he and Chris hit it off right away and worked together to infuse a higher standard of pride within the ranks. They concluded that one of the best ways to do that was through fitness. They led intense sessions daily before their formal SWAT training began.

"The guys were starving for that," Kevin said. "It filled a gap on SWAT that was distinctly Chris AuCoin." It also bred some friendly competition and became a mechanism to bond the guys tightly together.

"Man, just keep pace. You're right there with me." Kevin was a born runner and the 1.5 mile run for SWAT fitness testing was like zipping along on a spongy surface, he bounced along barely breaking a sweat. Chris, however, was confounded by his inability to overtake Kevin at the end. He'd keep up with him until the last few hundred meters, when Kevin would burst away and Chris would eat his dust.

"What the hell?" he'd come in, grabbing for air, deflated and annoyed. "What the actual hell?"

Kevin chuckled. He knew it bothered Chris to land anywhere below the number one position. Sure, he could whip by Chris in the fitness run, but no one came close in the gym. Chris could cleanly put up three hundred pounds on the bench. The spotter behind him never had to lift a finger. Over the course of his career in SWAT, Chris's noteworthy fitness, reputation for excellence, and earned respect among the guys pushed him higher. He saw a different path for the NHSP SWAT team and negotiated for state support to secure advanced training. In that, he and Kevin saw an opportunity to bypass some of the more senior guys on the team, who were less inclined to seek outside instruction. Kevin called it, common sense, but with more attached to it. Chris had a knack for working with the administration to smooth over whatever was necessary to move the team forward. His courage of conviction and natural aptitude for the job were unstoppable.

When Chris became Commander of the NHSP SWAT team, no one was prouder or less surprised than Kevin. Years later, everything he learned from Chris as his number two guy would be reflected in how he ran the team when it was his turn.

The overarching goal of any SWAT mission was centered around the preservation of life, preventing weapons engagement, softening an entry point, and luring a threat out. The most challenging and dangerous calls involved someone inside a house, armed with a weapon, and refusing to come out.

In October of 2007, Ed and Elaine Brown took that to a whole new level.

CHAPTER TWELVE
HEADS ON A SWIVEL

"They're getting close, guys," Chris told the SWAT team. "Close to bringing us in to get them. I think this will all come to a head soon. Eyes up and ready status."

Ed and Elaine Brown were notorious figures in an anti-tax crusade that earned them hero status among out-of-state militia groups. The shared mentality of that crowd attached its wagons to a belief that there was no legal justification for federal income taxes, nor the collection process of them. She, a practicing dentist in West Lebanon, and he an exterminator, together had amassed an arsenal of weapons, ammunition, and explosives on their Plainfield, New Hampshire property—a sprawling hundred-acres complete with a dwelling that resembled a fortress. A high tower broke the roofline into its own separate section with two levels of windows and a turret type dome. The Browns were refusing to pay their taxes and fell deeper into debt, which became the rally cry for what their twisted version of the state's motto: Live Free or Die, meant. They saw it as the perceived righteous campaign of their time. Most of the state saw it otherwise, this misuse considered to be egregious and grotesque, but the Browns determined they were willing to follow it word-for-word. Months went by as they took up positions in their dwelling and along their massive property, welcomed in waves of like-minded reinforcements—many skilled in war planning and prepared to defend the mission—and held off efforts by law enforcement who tried and failed to take the Browns into custody on federal charges.

The small, peaceful town of Plainfield was stressed as the atmosphere around the Brown property grew more tense and crowded. That summer felt like a circus of oddities, with bands setting up for live concerts, music pouring through the air—which ironically flowed across a dirt road where a summer home stood, one owned by then Supreme Court Justice Stephen Breyer. The Browns paid that distinction no mind and continued to garner the support of people who would show up with supplies that, according to news reports, included cell phones when the decision was made to cut power to the home and force them out. Strangers brought food and water, sustenance to keep the standoff funded with the basics. On and on it went, a gathering stormfront that threatened to burst. Federal agencies arrived on scene, set up a perimeter, and worked alongside local police. Unsustainable and dangerous, eventually Chris got the call to get his team ready.

The New Hampshire State Police SWAT team trained together for weeks. Staged at the armory in nearby Lebanon, Chris relayed updates as they came in to him.

"Okay, guys, word is the property is littered with booby traps and weapons. We should expect Brown supporters to be scattered through the woods. The entire place is set up to keep us out."

During Chris Vetter's early years alongside Chris AuCoin, he'd watched him rise from Assistant Commander of the NHSP SWAT, or the number two guy, to the top slot: Commander. When Vetter ran into AuCoin at the state police gun range one day, it was that conversation that prompted him to consider SWAT.

"I've heard about you," AuCoin told him. "Think you'd be a good fit."

It didn't matter if there were older guys on the team then, Chris AuCoin was in charge. Vetter called what Chris had a *presence.* Something so intangible it was impossible to explain, because Chris AuCoin was never gregarious. He simply walked in, looking like he was cut from granite, measured in how he spoke, and was always in charge.

That was his stance as Chris's team practiced and trained. Vetter and the rest of the SWAT team followed their commander's steady confident lead during the buildup to a final confrontation with the Browns. He'd already felt a natural inclination toward Chris, a gravitational pull born from a particular style of leadership. An innate ability to drop a bomb on a man when he needed it. Hold him accountable. As Vetter put it, Chris wasn't just a leader when the sun was out.

There was no space between expectations and Chris's sound preparation for his team during the Brown mission. He spent many nights at home studying every potential risk they might encounter out there in the woods. He pored over intel reports and replicated potential emergency situations if the team was ordered to advance beyond the perimeter.

Finally, Chris had called for them. The time was now.

"Not sure yet how, but we need to be prepared. It's probably going to be us." He never deployed lightly, only when necessary, and only when Chris felt prepared to keep every single one of them safe. *This,* the Browns, was not that. He was unsettled.

The pressure on the team with that pronouncement ratcheted up. They all gathered at the armory in nearby Lebanon, which served as the home base command center. Other agencies sprinkled into the area, all on comms and loudly working their own agendas. More days went by. Chris remained inside the command post monitoring developments. The team sat around and ate MREs out of squishy packages.

"Anyone want a beef stew?" they joked. "It's arguably the best option."

Mark Hall watched more than spoke. Among the younger guys on SWAT, he'd also been recruited onto the team by Chris. At first, Chris epitomized what a state trooper was to Mark, and when they'd first met at Troop B, Chris delivered impactful advice from day one. A mentorship position he naturally assumed, and when he called Mark out on something, it stuck.

"You're on the radar, buddy. Gotta get off the radar." Immediately, Mark would fix whatever Chris told him to. He felt fortunate, in that precarious situation in Plainfield, that Chris would never allow his team to be set up for failure. Much like Vetter, Mark absorbed Chris's confidence and made it his own. A love and respect earned when together, they stepped forth into danger.

Everyone mounted up on an armored truck. They drove from the armory toward the Brown compound. Chris Vetter and Mark Hall beside another SWAT member, who had been similarly recruited onto the team by Chris AuCoin. Sean Haggerty also considered Chris to be the premiere image of a professional state trooper, and when he suggested SWAT to Sean, he jumped, too. Sean also had young kids, like Chris, and felt honored to be taken under his giant wing—to learn process, procedure, and this hard job from the master.

They rode toward the Browns'.

Rolling through their minds on that ride was a review of goals to protect any civilian, especially when taking someone into custody. The Browns were considered *high end* targets because of their sophisticated weapons system and complex property. This wasn't one bad guy holed up in a house. No, this was a full slice of a small town, loaded with residents and risks—some potentially unknown—within a wide open, entirely uncontained swath of land. Sean saw that written all over Chris's face as they'd trained and the situation over at the property tensed. Along with the first point of this mission, protecting civilians, Chris's focus was also on keeping his team safe. Protect all law enforcement on scene. Sean knew Chris was doing fast math on assets, how many he needed to walk out of the woods once this thing was resolved. For a successful end to the incident, Chris had to protect his team from an obscure invisible enemy who could be positioned in front of, behind, or next to them at any moment.

Another mile to go.

The vastness of liability weighed on Chris—and his presence was felt right there with his team in that truck, bound for the Brown compound.

Chris addressed them on their radios with full honesty. The straight talk he was known to deliver, and what they expected.

"Okay, guys. Listen up." His voice boomed in from the command post. The truck rumbled along, its tires rolling over gravel and potholes. The guys' knees bobbed and spilled into each other's space; no one moved out of the way.

"We're going in and there's a good chance we're going to suffer casualties today," Chris started. All previous attempts to get Ed and Elaine Brown to peacefully exit their buttressed property had failed. It was SWAT's turn to raise the heat.

Vetter swallowed. It felt prickly as his nerves fired with the realization that Commander AuCoin would only say something that heavy if he believed it to be true. Any one of them could get shot. They could die out there. For the first time in his law enforcement career, the gravity of that spun around his stomach. That man did not deal in hyperbole. Life or death meant exactly that. He listened for more instructions and gripped his hands over his kneecaps. He felt Sean, seated next to him, elbows and legs touching, stiffen. Message received by all. This was unlike anything else they'd experienced as a team. Mark closed his eyes. He heard Chris in his own head, repeating to Mark how to operate once his armor was on.

Toughen up, compartmentalize. This was not trooper work often done autonomously, this was SWAT, and Chris expected Mark and every other man in that truck to be every bit the professional he'd trained them to be. He breathed deeply, calmly, and listened to his commander's voice on that radio.

"Likely advanced weapon systems within the property. Trip wires anticipated." Chris went on. "We'll enter through the woods a couple miles out. Be mindful of the multi-agency nature of this, a lot of other guys are already here. Keep your eyes up, head on a swivel. Always convey your location. They're probably waiting for us at the house."

The house, that had been turned into a military-style base camp, would be protected and defended. Built to be impenetrable. A proven complication for the extraction of the Browns, but there was more. Chris reminded them again of the dangers that awaited them before the house was even in sight.

"They want to intercept us on our way in," his voice metallically squelched from the box. That was in line with the training they'd been through and the various tactical options like dynamic entries, breaching, and flash bangs they could deploy to mitigate risks and injuries. "Expect hostiles upon approach. They have their own weapons and lookout points. They're watching and waiting for us. Targets may be deep in the house, protected with doors or barriers. Advance with expectation of hostiles everywhere and anywhere."

The team knew Chris had been in the planning and strategizing discussions as the multi-week buildup went on. A layered event with local and federal resources, it laid bare significant disadvantages his team would have if it were to be called in to wrangle the Browns from their standoff posture. Chris took that home every night. The pressure to purposely put himself and his men in a hot zone was relentless, and there was something even more sinister that Chris was dealing with as this case wore on. How it was impacting him personally. He never shared that with any of them as it unfolded.

The truck entered the staging position.

Chris worked with a desired outcome mindset and unrivalled focus on the moment-to-moment.

"Copy," he confirmed upon learning they'd arrived. He bowed his head, thinking, "Okay, here we go." While Chris had full confidence the guys would execute the mission—there was zero trust of it going by plan. There were too many variables at play. Sean, Chris Vetter, and Mark listened to their radios bleat out Chris's instructions. "Don't be exposed. Cameras in the woods."

They were all clocking the potential of casualties. In the command post, Chris communicated his concerns directly to his team, but he wasn't in charge of the overall operation, and being in a support role was irregular for him. It chafed against his voice in the relay of orders. Chris's mind whirled through what he was hearing in the command post and what his team needed to know.

"Heads on a swivel!" he told them again, mindful not to overwhelm but prepare. As always, he weighed his words and never spoke more than necessary. Those words, however, ran like a music bed through every second his guys were in the field.

This could go very bad. We could take fire. There may be casualties.

The strain rippled through the entire operation; the balance Chris had to strike between working collaboratively with other agencies and keeping his team safe to the extent that was at all possible.

"House in sight," the team relayed back to Chris.

"Copy. No exposure," he reminded them. Don't get seen.

They pushed forward.

Chris Vetter was tracking a new sound. He could hear banging. As if plywood was being hammered across windows in preparation of an assault. The Browns and their supporters locking themselves in.

"Jesus," he whispered to himself as he detected movement in his periphery and shifted his eyes to the right. He narrowed his view to get a better line of focus, signaling to the others around him with two fingers on his eyes and then on the potential hostile nearby.

The team moved through the woods, toward the figure, and radioed back to Chris. The closer they got, the team anticipated either taking out the hostile or eliminating even more threats. They stepped carefully around his position, half-expecting a wire to trigger a blast at any moment. One of them confirmed a weapon.

"Potential hostile armed. Rifle visible."

Their approach was calculated and careful and when the man positioned near a swamp finally heard them, he immediately put both hands up.

"Friendly!" he shouted. "ATF!"

It was the theme of the entire Brown operation. When Chris heard about the agent in the brush who'd failed to report his location, he was livid. Eventually, the standoff ended with little fanfare. US Marshals posing as Brown supporters entered the home and took them into custody. When Chris had a moment to speak at the command post, he ripped into the lead ATF agent for putting his men in danger.

"Count your men!" he roared. "Someone could've fired!"

When the Brown property was secured and searched, the full weight of the disaster that had been avoided was realized. The place was loaded with ammunition, sneaky traps that could maim or kill, and enough weapons to support a substantial firefight. Even years after Ed and Elaine Brown were sentenced to prison, their property sat empty—simply because it couldn't be fully determined that every booby trap, trip wire, or buried explosive had been neutralized.

The Browns and their supporters had strained all of them, particularly the NHSP SWAT team, and mostly Chris. What none of the guys knew at that time was why this case had become personal for him. Somehow, he'd been doxxed. Chris's address had been floated across the Brown's inner circle. Their crazed supporters knew Chris was the head of SWAT, but it was deeper and more troubling that just being a known target or a face in law enforcement.

They knew where Chris lived with his wife and children. The Browns had thrown a whole new variable at him—far beyond the risks Chris had accepted for himself as part of the job. Every time night fell in Plainfield, he could see Tracy in his mind, home alone, putting all three girls to bed, worried about him. Strong, but vulnerable, because evil always found ways to get in.

"Every call Chris went on; he tried to take in as much as he could. Every detail on a crime scene, an accident, whatever was going on. He thought it helped him become detached, to harden him in a way that made him more able to handle the job," Tracy explained. "He never looked away. But he also never wanted to tell me too much about what he'd seen. About the job."

What he'd seen in Plainfield was one thing, but the hypothetical was another. The threat to his family was insidious and tore at Chris's soul in unseen ways he never spoke of, but together with Tracy they planned for the unimaginable. She and Chris did what they had to do, but being a target out in the open was a game changer for all of them.

"I had to pull the girls out of school on multiple occasions. I'd go get them and take off. We thought about moving out of Wilton during that time. It rattled all of us."

Chris knew the risks and carried on with the job. To give his worst fears more power than what he could withstand was not part of his professional equation. Prepare, yet go forward remained the only option he could live with.

CHAPTER THIRTEEN
ENTANGLED

The behavior of the occupant on the first floor of an apartment building on Manchester's west side was trending in the wrong direction. The initial call that came in to police had reported some type of abuse allegation against a child, but it rapidly spun up from there. Juvenile detectives were brought in to speak with the man, learn more about what was going on inside, and check on the welfare of any children involved.

Knock, knock. "Manchester police, open up, we'd just like to talk."

The man opened the door and was immediately confrontational. Belligerent.

"Hey, hey, relax," the detectives tried to quiet him. "We just want to talk. We need to make sure everyone here is okay. You have any kids inside?"

The glint of a gun by the man's side caught their attention and the two detectives backed away from the open door. It shut behind them. They immediately let the OIC, or officer in charge back at the department, know what had just happened. With information now in hand that confirmed a weapon, and that a child inside was in danger, the decision to call in the Manchester Police SWAT team was made. It positioned and rolled toward the address.

Again, the man refused to let anyone in. Eight hours went by. Ten hours. Alan Aldenberg, eventual chief of the city's force, was, at that time, going to K-9 school and working on the Manchester SWAT team as a negotiator. His one goal was to protect the little kid and coax the armed man out. Attempts were made, but the man remained hostile. Unreachable at times.

"Just let us know you're okay. Talk to us." Aldenberg stood at a safe distance and used a bullhorn to be heard. He was trying to build this man's trust as police learned more about him and the relationship to the young child inside the apartment. Aldenberg had been on scene a long time, often going hours without any contact made. The man was holed deep inside and not willing to talk. An order came in for Aldenberg and the local SWAT team to be relieved. As is the case in multi-hour ongoing scenes, breaks must be taken, and reinforcements called. In this case, it was the NHSP SWAT team poised to replace Aldenberg and his fellow Manchester assets.

"Manchester has a situation," Chris told Kevin Duffy over the phone. "They've been working it all afternoon and then overnight, looking to rotate some people out."

Kevin listened to the details of the case, which were difficult and dangerous. Anytime someone was in a house and refusing to come out was bad. Throw in a child, and it gets exponentially worse. Civilians with the Department of Children Youth and Families had tried to remove this child, the Manchester police couldn't make any headway, and the hours wore on—which made the likelihood of a tragedy greater.

"Okay, Chris, on my way."

The NHSP SWAT team performed a tactical replacement on the perimeter and the negotiators swapped out. Aldenberg briefed his replacement on the status of communication with the suspect inside the house and left the scene. They did this swap out twice. Aldenberg returned and attempted another full round with the man. State police replaced them again. Negotiators continued to call for the man to talk. He stopped participating.

When Manchester was on scene, officers developed it enough to knock out a kitchen window and get visuals on the man inside and what the apartment looked like if an entry had to be forced. The information was shared with Chris and Kevin, who learned the main entrance had been barricaded.

"Problematic," Chris said to Kevin, next to him in the command post. He was concerned that if they had to breach to save the kid, all that junk was in their way.

"Yes."

They both felt that silent tension associated with the escalation of an incident. This had been going on for too long. The man was agitated, and no progress was being made to help that child. Something had to be done, and they both saw the broken kitchen window as a start. Chris assumed operational control as an armored vehicle was in position alongside the building. From his command post on the perimeter, Chris ordered his team inside the vehicle to move closer and examine what that barricade looked like if the moment came and they had no choice but to breach the entrance and rescue the child. Chris Vetter was inside the vehicle; holding one end of a long pole they'd attached a mirror to as it pulled up to the window. He positioned the pole so the mirror could reflect where the man was inside and get a better look. It was prudent to be prepared for what they'd encounter in a breach. The suspect was expecting them.

"Shit!" Vetter muttered as he saw the man in the mirror reach out his hands. "He's got the pole!" They struggled in a tug-of-war for control of the pole, the man now wide open for them all to see. In the back and forth, the mirror slammed into the armored vehicle, its abrupt connection with the hardened side giving off a sound indistinguishable from the one a gun would make when the trigger was pulled.

Believing they were being fired upon, SWAT fired back. Two rounds ripped through the man's chest and then struck the fridge behind him in the kitchen. Vetter, and the rest of the team jumped from the armored vehicle, through the broken window, and into the apartment. The child was found safe in another room.

Thirty-five hours after it started, the NHSP SWAT team was in position when it ended. And there were questions to be answered. Vetter and the rest of the team reported back to Chris that the man fired on them, they fired back, counted all their rounds, and most of all, felt enormous relief that the child was safe. But it was the first deadly encounter for NHSP SWAT in many years. Chris, as commander, bore the heaviness of that.

Once the team was cleared from the scene, Kevin took them all out for breakfast. Sitting around the table at a diner, they further discussed the pole, mirror, and the exchange of bullets. Chris Vetter, who'd acted as the sub leader on the team, sipped on hot coffee and listened intently to something that sounded odd. As did Kevin.

"Wait a minute," Kevin stopped one of the team members mid-sentence. "Start over."

"After we dropped the guy and he was taken out of the apartment, his gun was in his waistband."

Kevin rolled his tongue over his back teeth, nodded. "Tell me again. Slowly."

The statement, even on low speed, remained the same. The suspect, shot and killed after firing at them, was taken out of the apartment with his gun in the waistband of his pants. All at once, they fell into a hushed quiet, realizing there was no way a dead guy could have fired his gun, absorbed two bullets and simultaneously returned that weapon to his pants.

"Shit!" Kevin flew from the table. He had to tell Chris.

—★—

Chris clicked off the call with Kevin and knew what he had to do next. The state prosecutor on the case was about to brief the press on the deadly end to the standoff, but he didn't have the facts. Chris had to set that straight. The call with the prosecutor was tense and Chris weathered the heat in his customary calm and controlled manner. When pressed about how such a misstatement could've been made, how in the world NHSP SWAT mistook a banging mirror for a gunshot, he was protective but honest. In the haze of war, details tended to get blurry, which they had in this case. Chris accepted the correction would be all his to make, as would the examination of the incident. He shouldered it all.

"Would you rather have the correct info before your brief?" he asked. "If it were me, I'd rather go out there knowing exactly what happened. What I just told you is exactly what happened."

The pivot was effective in the moment, but it was a tough position for Chris. While deadly force had been authorized in a shoot-on-site sort of way to protect an innocent, they always preferred non-deadly outcomes, Chris especially, given he led their training. As the dust settled on Main Street in Manchester, the family would later tell reporters the child inside was the dead suspect's daughter, and had been moved away to a separate room when he was shot. They also claimed he'd never do anything to hurt her. Emotions and facts easily entangled into a story that must have felt preferable for that family to tell.

Alan Aldenberg confirmed every procedure to self-report the shooting went by the book, and that the father holed up inside with his daughter was likely the type who'd never release her simply because he wasn't man enough to face what was about to rain down on him. During the endless hours trying to talk that man down, Aldenberg had worried about that little girl, an innocent pawn in all of it, and the pressure he felt that she could be harmed while they were being kept outside. It had worn on him and the Manchester team like a weight vest. He'd exchanged intel with Chris in the command post during the asset exchange with NHSP SWAT and appreciated his no-nonsense demeanor. Aldenberg would hear of him again many years later, when the dam holding Chris together, was starting to buckle. Because much like the stories some people chose to share, police work could also become so entangled it, too, was suffocating.

—★—

Mark Hall felt a growing comfort with SWAT, and much of that was because of Chris. He and the team performed exceptionally well for Chris, because they knew he took the brunt for them with state administration—and none of them wanted to be the root cause of anything extra for their commander to deal with.

Along with the Brown standoff, the NHSP SWAT team was called to Boscawen early in Mark's career for another risky intervention. Chris briefed them on what was going on in the town just north of Concord, the state's capital and where much of NHSP's work was centered. Mark's pulse quickened on the information. This was a highly volatile situation. It was a late Friday afternoon, and the sun would set soon. Things tended to get hairy at nighttime. Reports of a shooting had come in over a custody dispute between parents. Two people had been shot.

"Okay, here's what we know." Chris told the team about shots fired, two down. The couple's child was being held hostage inside the house. "Negotiators are talking to the guy, let's give that some time, but not too much. I will green light a breach when it's clear. Wait for my call."

Mark and the others assembled into a quick reaction position outside the home's attached garage. They'd already been told to stand down a couple of times when the man's son came to the screen inside the front door and called out to police.

"Come on in and help me!" he said, but his voice was flat, more matter of fact, less panicked. The team was perched on that invisible line. The child was right there!

"No, no, no!" Chris yelled over comms. "Do not go! We're being baited!"

It was one of the hardest orders to give and follow. The team could be in the door in mere seconds to pluck that little boy out. To save him from the horrors of what was inside. Mark held his position because Chris had ordered him to. The team exchanged glances, though their eyes remained trained on that door. On that boy.

More negotiations failed. The boy's father, deeper inside the house, had stopped answering. Just as Chris was about to give SWAT the green light to enter the house, the boy stepped out of the front door. Mark's heart slammed against his ribs and his eyes blinked, trying to make sense of what he was seeing. Everyone moved. They moved so fast he didn't wait for his brain to decode what his eyes were relaying back to it. Suddenly, it was clear exactly what they were seeing.

The boy walked a few more steps. Staggered and stood still. He was shirtless. A wetness that looked almost black was spreading across his chest, and if he'd turned around his back would have shown the same. Mark felt motion by his arm as Sean Haggerty flew by him, grabbed the boy and cradled him between his outstretched arms. He took off, sprinting down the road to an awaiting ambulance.

"I got him!" he screamed. "I got him!"

Mark's breath was clipped, quickened by such rapid-fire developments.

"He was shot; he was shot." The words tumbled out, in some way grounding them in a moment that didn't feel real. "He shot that kid. He shot his own son."

One by one, the SWAT team debriefed Chris. Vetter gruffly rubbed a hand over his face as the sound of the child, bleeding in Sean's arms, that gurgle of agonizing pain and his small body's emotional destabilization played on repeat in his mind. He'd also had the father right there—in his scope, 40 yards out. Chris, not giving him permission to shoot.

"Do not get baited!" he told them, repeatedly. "We go in, someone could get shot!"

They learned the man inside, that father, had stabbed himself after hurting his son and was dead. Chris laid one of his big hands on Mark's shoulder. He squeezed. Chris was not to be questioned, even though Mark had nothing but worrisome questions on his mind. Had he failed? Had Mark failed to rescue that boy? What if he'd moved sooner? What ifs collected behind a cloud that Mark felt suspended in. He couldn't move out of its way, so it absorbed him in its painfully intoxicating fullness. Chris squeezed his shoulder again.

"Now you listen to me," he declared. "I told you not to go. I did not give you the green light to go in. It was not safe for me to send you in. Understand? That kid was not believable, and I wasn't about to risk your life. You listened to me. You followed my orders. Nothing here is your fault."

Mark nodded, but with a numbness he couldn't shake for a long time. He wasn't equipped then with any mechanism to find his way back below that cloud, but he did descend eventually. Mark dealt with it in his own way. Chris checked in on every member of SWAT after that incident and made sure each was okay before any of them left the scene and returned home that night.

The guys on the team supported each other but didn't always talk about it. In their hard-charging, tough group, Chris never let on that anything was bothering him. Mark watched and replicated Chris's style of leadership and trusted it. The quietly humble demeanor and deep confidence Chris had in himself and each of them. He made his own peace with that night in Boscawen and placed his life in Chris's hands many more times. When he checked in on Mark, or stopped by just to talk, the love and respect between them was earned and reciprocated. Often, Mark would share a bit of his work with his wife, who like Tracy, had been a dispatcher. Mark felt lucky to love a woman who innately knew what his heart needed after such a disastrous night at work. He talked with her, and she helped him find clearer air—beneath the cloud.

Chris wasn't like that, though. Instead of baring his emotions to Tracy or anyone, he put all his burdens away inside himself. He never made excuses for that; it was just who he was. Astutely and authentically himself on every occasion, Chris had been shaped by a personal alignment of values, tastes, and truths. And while he never sought to be understood, reinvented, or dissuaded—his life wasn't built on avoidance, nor was he manufactured or curated by some shiny new theory or talking point. He was a brand unto himself, and his genuineness made that stick.

The Rock.

While Chris checked in on all of them, Mark couldn't recall if anyone ever checked in on him.

CHAPTER FOURTEEN
EXTREME ACTS

Chris shuffled through the NHSP leadership hierarchy at a swift pace. From his first job at Troop B and subsequent roles as Field Training Officer during his early years in SWAT, to being transferred to Troop C and promoted to Staff Sergeant as the Assistant Troop Commander, he was personally close to many of his SWAT teammates and NHSP colleagues, often meeting up for cookouts or get-togethers on the weekends. At work, Chris was the pristine representation of a serious, locked-in professional, but at home, he could be a goof. As the father of three girls, Chris was often wrapped in pink boas, his pinky up as he sipped imaginary tea from a delicate cup, or rolled around on the floor in a tickle fight. One night in 2009, he came home from one of the most atrocious calls he'd ever been on—and may have stood in the doorway of his daughters' rooms staring at their slumbering faces until dawn broke on some other family's most devastating day.

Chris seemed to find a place in himself that could shuffle into different modes. The work Chris and the family Chris. The ratio wasn't always even, however, and work tugged and pulled in that relentless, all-consuming sort of way. Chris loved being a dad, but felt like law enforcement was his life calling—and he was as protective of his daughters as he was of the men and women who served beneath him. No one realized more than he that all of it—the kids, the wife, the beautiful house and fun toys in the driveway—could all be gone in a day.

A second.

Life was fragile, and Chris's career in law enforcement epitomized how instantly everything can change.

—★—

Chris Vetter had grown up in Greenland, New Hampshire, about 500 yards from one of the worst police disasters in the state's history. He was picking up his kids in nearby Dover when the initial blast of information started coming in. Right from the start, the 2012 incident in Greenland was a disaster. A deadly, awful, heartbreaking mess.

Sirens, dozens of them, shrilled through the crisp April air as the sun cast long shadows through the budding tree limbs. The cacophony of alarm, deafening and dramatic, indicative of some massive thing. The biggest that small town had ever experienced, and certainly one that reached into the hearts of law enforcement figures nationwide. Greenland, New Hampshire was now the latest dot on the map for all the wrong reasons.

The town's police chief had joined officers from his department and the Attorney General's Drug Task Force in the execution of a search warrant. The local home was quiet at first as they exited their vehicles in a circular driveway and moved toward the door. The subject inside was suspected of drug activity, and known to police for being volatile and, at times, violent. As the group strode to the door, the clock ticked just past six o'clock. The sun dipped lower. Dinner time. They were all expected home soon, loved ones waited for their return. The chief would join his wife later, right after he'd wrapped up the warrant.

Mere minutes after the group approached the home's front door to conduct the search, Chris sent out a text to SWAT: **Respond immediately**. Chris Vetter, who knew that house, road, and police chief very well, immediately spun around, and raced home to drop off his kids. He called Chris.

"What do we know?" he asked him on his way back.

"Guy's holed up. No one left to transport out, the yard is clear. Officers down." They knew that much, but little else about what the standoff would demand, if the man inside the house was willing to come out on his own or not. "Bad, bad scene," Chris told Vetter. He knew it was likely to be a long night ahead of them. "Get your gear, come right back. I'll be there."

Chris never built scenarios in his head prior to landing on an active scene, preferring to plan around firm facts as they evolved. There were certain aspects of SWAT that were constant and proven, but the criminally deranged could be fluid and unpredictable. What he knew before taking control of that operation was that a subject had open fired during the warrant delivery, officers were dead, and his guys may have to go in and get the shooter out of the house. In the command post at a nearby school, Chris was in charge, even as the room filled with high-ranking state leaders, including the governor and commissioner of the NHSP. As the hours wore on, Chris was inundated with suggested tactical scenarios, particularly one that had SWAT entering the home, likely absorbing gunfire on the way in, and overtaking the suspect inside. Chris called Vetter.

"It's what they want us to do. You know and I know we'd probably get shot. It's a bad idea."

Vetter understood Chris was relaying his position on breaching the house up the chain of command, that he was refusing to put his team in the direct line of fire.

"Find another way," he had told Vetter. "Do what you can do to put that down."

The team was in the armored BEAR vehicle on the perimeter of the rainbow-shaped driveway. The suspect's vehicle was positioned directly in front of the steps that led to the door. SWAT couldn't bypass the car in the BEAR to more safely enter the house. Vetter called Chris.

"What are you seeing?" Chris asked him.

"Car's blocking entry, impeding us from getting in. We want to move the car."

Chris weighed the scene conditions. The car blocked the door. The suspect had stopped communicating. SWAT could face fire if they tried to move the car themselves. He heard conversations around him, and a rising pressure to send his guys in. The hours stretched on, the gunman inside was no longer responding to calls being made from the outside. Chris maintained his team's position until early the next morning.

"We gotta move the car." Vetter gave Chris the option, the *other way* they preferred.

"Do it," Chris told him. "Use the BEAR."

The battle rig rolled forward and used an exposed ram to push the suspect's vehicle. Its tires rocked with the pressure to move, but it didn't take much to scoot it out of the way. SWAT had a clear view of the front door. It was quiet inside, but that meant nothing. The suspect could be positioned in a window, behind a curtain, gun aimed and tracking their approach. They got their first confirmed look at him, and a woman, by way of a robot equipped with a video camera. It entered first and provided reconnaissance that organically yielded an end to the hellish event. The suspect was dead along with the woman who'd been with him inside the house.

Vetter relayed everything back to Chris at the command post. "Deceased. Two deceased."

It was nearly four in the morning by the time the call concluded, and the house had been secured. Local reporters clamored for updates, and Chris managed what was released to the public from the command post, standing by his decision to crush the car to keep his men out of that house. Vetter returned to the BEAR, sat down and took stock of the long night. As the adrenaline wave leveled out, he noticed a local police chief he knew well inside the vehicle. He'd been there, on that scene, for hours just as SWAT had. His eyes were tired, but there was a bewildered defoliation brewing. A new reality his mind was vehemently working to section off, because to absorb it whole was too thick to conceive of. His head hung low as Vetter watched nearby. All at once, in the aftermath of pandemonium, he saw it. A pain so pronounced and inflexible it felt almost otherworldly, like a portal to a parallel new world had just opened wide and it was too dark to see a way forward. How did anyone survive that place? Vetter went to hug the police chief who had just lost his best friend.

"I'm so sorry," he whispered.

Greenland hurt like hell because the cruelest irony had struck down upon the town's police chief while it still could—as if it had calculated that the time to make its move was about to expire.

After a long and distinguished career in the military and law enforcement, the Greenland police chief who'd chosen to attend the search warrant execution in his hometown was eight days away from retirement. When all the crews pulled out of the town and resumed the gritty work their career demanded, it stood as a stalwart example that it could have been any of them, either now… or later.

—★—

Joe Ebert crossed paths with Chris often, and in different professional capacities. When he was a coming up as a SWAT negotiator, and later in the state's Major Crime Unit, Chris was often the highest-ranking leader on a scene or case. In fact, Joe knew Chris in the context of New Hampshire's most violent cases. In 2006, Joe was brought in to communicate with a woman in Franklin who had just shot a store owner, left his bloody body on the sidewalk in front of it, and climbed the stairs to her apartment on the second floor of the building. She'd been holding off police for over nine hours, luring them closer, and according to witnesses, was willing to let any of them fire back and take her out.

As SWAT assembled outside the building, Chris was focused on preservation of life. The man's body was sprawled on the ground, but he needed more confirmation.

"We need to rescue him if he's still alive," he told the team. "We're going in to check."

At the same time Chris got his team prepared to move, Joe watched each member follow Chris's lead. He wasn't part of their group, men who wove themselves around each other to move as one, so intuitively attached to a singular intent they inherently shared the same wavelength. Joe stayed behind on the perimeter, his role as communicator all but over by then, as Chris made that call. *Wow,* he thought, *they're really going to walk in there to try and save that guy.* Chris knew their movement onto the sidewalk, with the woman positioned high above in a window, might force a deadly encounter. His men were in a direct line of fire, powerless to avoid escalation, yet Chris had to choose. Save the life of an innocent or keep his men away. In the trajectory of priorities, the injured man on the sidewalk ranked highest. Chris knew that. SWAT knew that. He made the call to send his guys right into the kill zone with full confidence it was the right thing to do.

"Get the medic over there. Confirm victim status."

Vetter and the other SWAT members huddled behind protective shields and moved through the exterior.

"Eyes on the window! Who's tracking the window?!"

They had to pass immediately below the window where the woman was firing. Miraculously, SWAT was able to get the medic close enough to the man's body to confirm he was dead.

"Deceased." SWAT confirmed back to Chris.

"Get out, get out, get out!"

"Copy."

SWAT reported back to a more secure position along the building's yard. Nighttime gave way to the hushed pink hues of the rising sun. The woman decided that was the time to give up. She exited the house without any further loss of life.

Joe watched this woman being taken into custody, the drawn expressions of the SWAT team, and Chris—who tried, but couldn't save the shop owner. He'd operated under extreme peril to his beloved guys who'd had to go in almost bare. It hit him, that level of responsibility Chris had shouldered that night, to be the one who called the plan that was potentially risky at best, but deadly at worst.

It was astounding, Joe thought, how Chris never wavered. There, in Franklin, or elsewhere. Chris could reset on a scene almost instantaneously, but the safety of his crew mattered in every decision he made. He called it top of mind for Chris to protect his team.

Joe was often included in Chris's debriefs, too. When he'd gather up everyone who'd reported to him during an incident, some which had ended in a less-than-ideal manner. At times, portions of the response were critically analyzed—those split-second decisions that fell on Chris, questioned. The times he ordered his team into danger because he had to, or when other tactics failed and limited options were left on the table, subject to dismantle and review. Chris agreed they should be.

"We do not operate in a clean environment," he told them. "These are dirty decisions we make to preserve life." Chris stood there like a planted tree, his enormous biceps and arm veins popping. He was honest yet protective. The noise on the outside could be deafening if they let it in.

"I know every one of you did the right thing, everything you possibly could to resolve this. But when we are brought in to execute a dirty task, it is not reasonable to come out clean."

Those were hard talks to deliver, and they meant a lot to Joe, who was still building his career and considered Chris a profoundly transformational figure in his life. A leader who supported the guys whenever they were being questioned. He'd tell whoever was asking, 'hey, you put them into this terrible situation, they did the best they could. Sometimes things don't work out the way you hoped they would.' And sometimes, Chris was the only one who never gave up on any of them.

SWAT couldn't save everyone. When a patrol officer was ambushed while responding to a domestic call in Brentwood, his body locked in the house as pressure built on Chris to send his team in to retrieve it, he pushed back against the clear threat to life.

"We're not going anywhere," he told the officials trying to force him to do otherwise. "It is not safe for my guys. I trust what they're telling me, and it's a no on entry."

Vetter and Kevin Duffy kept Chris in the loop of what they saw and heard from their position around that house. Pops of gunfire, a visible head shot to the officer seen through a window.

"We are confident he is dead. Confirm, officer inside is dead."

But the pressure to act simmered, the heat climbing on Chris.

"Copy," Chris relayed back to his team. "Don't worry about this here," he told them from the command post, knowing they were aware of calls to breach the house. "Let me worry about that. Hold positions outside."

Chris trusted his team above all else, and it returned that trust tenfold. The Brentwood standoff ended in a spectacular ball of fire ignited by explosives the suspect set on the inside. Chris ran the entire operation that day and then stayed on in the days ahead to cover the funeral of the officer so every other member of law enforcement could attend. He oversaw everything, and no one ever thought it should be any other way.

CHAPTER FIFTEEN
FRACTURES

By 2012, Chris had received what would be his final promotion within NHSP, when he was elevated from captain to major. His career had spanned two decades by then, and Chris had held every leadership role the state's rank structure offered, except one. With his eyes now set on the only remaining slot as a potential goal, Chris discussed what that life may look like with his family. None of them doubted Chris's fitness to serve as colonel, but they began to see unsettling developments in his behavior. While he maintained his physical strength and prowess, and looked the same as he always had, something was stirring on the inside. Something disturbing and unfamiliar to who Chris had been his entire life.

Brent remembers it succinctly; the exact moment he knew Chris was different. Sometimes, it's subtle like the unhurried decline of temperature during the darkening skies of a late fall afternoon. Other times, it's abrupt and so obviously a departure of the norm, it gets stuck in your memory like a frozen weathervane. What had always pointed due north was suddenly spinning in the wind.

Brent had taken a job with the state and within the structure of his new role with the Department of Safety, Brent now answered to Chris.

They'd joked about that juxtaposition of power, but Brent appreciated a new access point into Chris's life. Seeing him every day at work was reconnecting them in ways Brent hadn't been granted since Chris joined the Marines and moved out of their family home. Many times, they'd find a remote area in the building they both worked in and have lunch together. But this one day, Brent watched Chris as he pulled apart a sandwich.

"Maybe stop playing with it, and just eat it, Chris," Brent suggested with a smirk. "It's just bread."

But Chris picked around. "Dad, there's mold here. I'm trying to cut the mold away."

Brent stopped chewing and stared at him. "Come again?"

"Mold." Chris looked at him with a hardness, as if to suggest Brent was being patently ignorant of the issue. "There's mold on the bread, Dad, and I have to cut it off."

Brent's mouth opened. He tried to rattle a response, but his whole body felt chilled. He'd shared investment strategies with Chris through the years as his paycheck and opportunities had grown. Brent had dabbled in real estate ventures and taught his sons how to make their money work for them. How to take care of their families first and secure their financial future with smart spending and forward-thinking growth. This mold hunting felt like Chris was taking Brent's sensible advice and morphing it into the absurd.

"I think you're taking frugal a bit too far, Chris," he managed. "What's wrong with buying a new loaf of bread?"

Then, the phone calls started. "Hi, Brent, have you seen Chris today?"

The colonel of the New Hampshire State Police was also noticing some oddities. Certainly, Chris felt an obligation to be out in the field with his teams and would routinely pop in at various troops across the state to check in and punch some clock. He wanted to be seen and create an atmosphere of accessibility. But the colonel was made aware of blatant absences, lapses of time when Chris couldn't be reached. Paula had some insight as Chris would share with her things he wouldn't tell his dad.

"It's this desk job," she told Brent. "Chris is having a hard time with it. It's completely out of character for him to be sitting all day."

While Chris never admitted he was truly troubled, he had discussed a new development with his mom. An anxious sensation he attributed to being still, not on the move like he was used to. He told Paula how strange it felt to downshift from making moment-to-moment, life or death decisions, to shuffling paperwork around a desk in an administrative role.

"It's unnatural for him," she continued. "Chris needs to be moving."

Brent agreed. And while Chris relished the expansion of responsibility in his career, the job requirements were hampering every instinct he'd accrued along the way. To see a scene with his own eyes, be among his team, lead from a position of proximity with intimate knowledge of an operation and assets. That was where Chris shined.

"Brent, is something going on with Chris?" the colonel pressed. Regardless of Chris's stellar career, there were too many flags being raised at work that couldn't be ignored or kicked down the road. When a state investigator pulled Brent into a room one day and started firing questions at him, he answered truthfully.

"Do you know where Chris is?"

"No, not always," Brent replied.

"Is he drinking? Is he struggling with alcohol?"

"Not that I know of."

"Can you think of any reason why Chris wouldn't show up for work?"

Brent paused. He knew Chris enjoyed a drink occasionally, just as he did. Many times, when they were together out of work, they'd crack a few beers and relax. Had something changed? Was Chris drinking more than Brent knew? He never suggested that to the investigator, but it lingered there in the room. That impossible question.

"No. I have no idea why Chris wouldn't show up for work." While it was the truth, the gray areas in Brent's mind were rapidly expanding.

—★—

In 2001, Brent and Paula bought a home in Vero, Florida, and spent a good chunk of time away from New Hampshire as Chad attended flight school down south. While they often flew home to check in on Chris, Tracy, and their girls, there were stretches of time when Chris was quiet and they didn't hear much from him. Tracy would only call them if circumstances were dire, and much of what was unfolding with Chris like the first few raindrops of a monsoon was not clear to them. During a trip back home shortly after Chris was promoted, trouble rolled in on two wheels.

"But Chris. Why? Why in the world?" Paula stood dumbfounded in Chris's driveway in Wilton, her arms crossed over her chest like a self-hug.

"Just wanted it," Chris told his parents. "So, I got it."

Brent stifled a pained chuckle as he walked around the brand-new Harley Davidson, sitting there in Chris's garage like a white ghost. He chuckled again in consternation. This bike, this feminine-looking beast was, at least aesthetically, so antithetical to Chris it was impossible to apply rationale. And the cost! Not long ago Chris had been snipping mold off his bread, but now he was okay with cutting a check for this monstrosity. Brent's eyes met Paula's and the look they shared felt like impending doom. It made no sense. Chris was a planner. He was meticulous with his money and investments and had never spoken about a desire to buy a motorcycle. With three young daughters, it also seemed somewhat irresponsible to them—but any mention beyond what Chris had already explained was not welcomed, nor elaborated upon.

Chris wanted it, so he got it.

"They rode dirt bikes as kids," Brent reminded Paula during a strained ride back home. "He and Nate had that boat, remember? He does like having toys."

Paula nodded, her hands tightly wound together in her lap. Chris primarily used the boat once Nate's construction career took off.

"But this is different. It's not like when they were kids," she clarified. "It's this spending on himself," she said. "That isn't Chris."

The Chris they were used to was on a constant prowl for investments that would return value for his family. This white Harley wasn't a fit in that way, but it went way beyond one atypical purchase. Chris followed up the motorcycle with a huge tractor that appeared one day and his response to why he needed one, particularly of that caliber and price tag, was as simple as before.

"I wanted it, so I got it." He shrugged away his parent's bewilderment as though it was superficial and unimportant to him. The tractor, as majestic as the white Harley, was blinking out red warning lights and everyone could see them but Chris.

"It's like that song," Paula told Brent during another strained drive from Wilton back to Jaffrey.

"Which one?"

Paula's eyes went hot with tears. "That Tim McGraw song. You know. Live like you were dying. It's what he's doing."

Brent couldn't tell her she was wrong.

—★—

As it often tends to do, illness came in silently, stealth-like, a thief and scoundrel that leached the strength and power it would need to collapse the natural rhythm of wellness from a human body. It came for Chris.

Brent and Paula sat with him and Tracy, shocked into a somber quiet as Chris explained the treatment plan for his newly diagnosed thyroid cancer.

"Surgery will be in May," he told his parents. "I'll be fine. Maybe just a few weeks of figuring out all the stuff."

Stuff meant the post-op healing, and a smattering of pills Chris would need to take. A full pharmaceutical replacement of every hormone his thyroid once regulated would become a synthetic placeholder. And that would take some trials and errors—none of which sounded good to Brent and Paula. Tracy, armed with her nursing knowledge, knew the next year or so would be challenging, but the middle brother, Nate, noticed a sharp decline in Chris immediately. It wasn't just the new toys in the garage. There was an edginess chafing around Chris's head, as though he was fighting off a perpetual state of fever. But this. This diagnosis and its aftermath were about to tear him apart, and Nate felt that in his bones.

Chris made it a point to go speak to Nate in person, to tell him about the upcoming surgery, and what he'd be dealing with to get better. He arrived at Nate's house, and they spent some time talking. They'd weathered many incidents, these two, but to Nate, Chris was always the big brother, and they stuck together while growing up, even when that wasn't easy to do. Nate pushed boundaries and flexed his wild side, which often put him directly in his brother's crosshairs.

"Jesus, Nate," Chris had admonished years before after his brother had caused a roadblock incident in Merrimack or induced a high-speed chase through nearby towns. "You gotta knock this off. I can't be chasing you around. Stop causing trouble!" Long before full adulthood had kicked in for Nate, he and Chris had come to an understanding. They were very different and would accept each other as such.

As Nate digested Chris's news, he turned his body into his brother's and wrapped himself around his barrel chest. Nate had him by height, but Chris's girth and firmness filled his arms. Without thinking, Nate kissed his neck. Chris wasn't having it.

"Jesus Christ, what the hell?" The shove to Nate's chest felt like a sledgehammer had just landed between his ribs. "What are you doing, man?"

Nate's voice was low. "I don't know, Chris. I just wanted to do that."

He didn't tell his brother about the feeling that had crept in, or that it told him that Chris was never going to be the same. While he and Chris had always maintained the ability to get over a squabble within minutes after it had erupted, cancer broke their record. 2013 became known as the year it all went bad. The entire family marked a new and calamitous chapter of their lives.

Not long after Chris had major surgery to remove his thyroid, he asked Brent to spend some time with him at his rental property in Old

Orchard Beach, Maine. Whenever Chris was in a state of unrest, he'd begun to spend time away from Tracy and the girls in Wilton, squirreling himself into this beach house, which seemed to help calm his post-surgical uneasiness. The visit wasn't intended to be restful or even aid in his recuperation, instead, Chris needed Brent's help with a heavy and laborious project.

"See all these windows?" Chris asked Brent, pointing to the wood rot along the edges of the home's upstairs windows. Time, sea air, and condensation were licking away at the boards, and the glass was starting to break down after years of exposure to humidity and beating sunlight. "They're fogging, Dad. And I think the seals are failing, there are gaps here where the air is getting in."

Brent could see where condensation was streaking on the inside face of the glass and distorting the view. Although the timing was poor, with Chris still healing from a wide scar just above his collarbone and beneath his Adam's apple, and his medications altering his metabolism and body functions, he was adamant on making the window repair that day. He was not to be swayed into waiting. Brent was uncomfortable with the irrationality of Chris's obstinance and tried talking him out of the job.

"Chris, let's hold on this for a few more weeks. This is a big job, even with me here to help. I'm worried you could hurt yourself."

It was useless. Chris refused to listen to his dad's reasoning, but he did forgo the windows in favor of another project, one equally as physically demanding. When Brent arrived back at the Maine house days later, he found Chris digging narrow trenches to replace sections of the fence.

"I'm fine, Dad. I'm doing this now. You can help, or you can go home, and I'll do it myself."

They faced each other as Brent's protestations failed, and Chris grew more tense. From a psychological standpoint, Brent knew he was on one side of a stalemate but what he couldn't yet see was the internal skirmish his son was having with himself. His storied state police career and reputation built upon an impenetrable strength of body and mind, was fractured. He had cracked. A disease had poked a hole through Chris's armor, and for the first time in his life, Chris experienced a vulnerability. He was not made of brick and intensely angry about that.

Brent helped Chris replace the fence posts and heard an audible pop as his son was navigating boards and punching through the ground.

"Oh, God!" he yelled, horrified that his premonition was unfolding in real time. Chris was hurt. As fresh blood pooled around the incision on his neck, Chris continued working.

"Nah, I'm fine. I'm good, Dad."

Brent drove home in a tormented daze. A baseball-sized mass had formed under Chris's skin, even as he'd whisked his father out the door and promised to have it looked at.

He wasn't sure that was a promise Chris had any intention of keeping. Tracy interceded.

"He was in so much pain," she told Brent and Paula.

While Chris didn't want to take pills, he couldn't stand the pain.

Tracy got him Boston and took him home with a prescription from the doctor. Then, she helped wean him off the pills.

But there was still the drinking to contend with.

CHAPTER SIXTEEN
DUST UPS

"Kevin, I'm calling you…"

Tracy's voice trailed off. She'd called Kevin Duffy and then gone quiet when he'd picked up.

"Tracy, is everything okay?" he asked, immediately on edge. Chris had shared with him how awful he'd been feeling after thyroid surgery, telling him he was out of whack. Not right. It wasn't just the recovery or the meds; Chris seemed to be caught in a full body system chaos he couldn't pull out of. Months went by. Medications were adjusted. Nothing could shake him back.

"Chris is here with me in the car."

Kevin's impeccably developed instincts were on par with Chris's, and he sensed this call from Tracy might be something akin to a line drawn in the sands of time. For some reason he didn't yet know, Kevin felt as though that moment, Tracy's call, would be a core memory in his life. He gently asked Tracy again if everything was okay.

"Well…" she started.

Kevin heard a shuffling sound, a sudden movement around the phone. Then, Chris's booming voice.

"Hey, Kev. All good here. We're fine. No issues."

Kevin kept his voice calm and steady. While he had no idea what was really happening, he needed to stay cool.

"Chris, you okay, man? What's going on?"

"Nothing, bud. We're good here."

And then he hung up.

—★—

Chris's commander during his deployment for Desert Storm would eventually move his family to the beautiful Lakes Region of New Hampshire. Having weathered some of his own post-deployment hyper-vigilance, Phil Smith needed a spatial withdrawal from society to feel more secure. He found that by way of mountain views and the cool, clean water of the state's largest lake. He'd also achieved the highest level of his aviation career and was working as a pilot for United Airlines. Phil's life was full, and he was content—but around the time Chris went through thyroid cancer, he was worried his former Marine was not having an easy go of it. Even as Chris was worried about him.

"I'm scared for you, sir. You're going to get this, too!"

Phil could hear the fear in Chris's voice. He was in hyper-drive, near panicked.

"Please, sir, please go get yourself checked out. Please make sure you're okay."

The advice from Chris was sound and the risk, real. Phil knew better than most what they'd been exposed to over there trudging through desert minefields and the decay of battle. Their boots encased with spent uranium and shells, their bodies and skin absorbing poison. Chemical detectors going off at all hours. Chris was convinced the contamination had caused his cancer. Phil didn't try to tell him otherwise, though he did reach out more often to check in.

They'd maintained a unique sort of connection through the years, and when Chris trained for his pilot's license, Phil was an obvious conduit to that world above the clouds.

But in the one down below, where they all lived full-time, Chris's senses and abilities to find an opening to descend back where he used to be kept misfiring. He remained sky-high. Phil had never seen Chris take a drink before thyroid cancer. Now he was getting calls from Brent, Paula, and his Marine brothers Buddy Hackett, and Kevin Sullivan telling him Chris was on another bender and could he help reel him back in.

—★—

New Hampshire State Police Captain Greg Ferry had heard rumblings within the upper echelon of leadership. There was something going on with Major AuCoin, and that didn't jibe with the Chris he knew.

Greg first saw Chris at the Southern New Hampshire University pool when both were training for the state trooper exam. Along with the written portion of the test, all candidates had to pass a swim test that included laps and treading water.

Greg called Chris a total stud, and even as they sized each other up during that initial meeting, he knew Chris would make it through. He looked ready, focused, and while they never spoke to each other, Greg thought Chris looked like a trooper long before he was one.

He and Greg became friends during their time at Troop B. Chris was already highly respected there, and Greg noticed how that style of substance over splash he'd first seen at the SNHU pool was Chris's signature theme. Nothing ruffled him, he was never rattled or out of control. Chris had a command presence Greg considered to be perfect, with his leadership entirely calm and present. When Greg crossed paths with Chris, they always paused to chat.

"Hey, man, keep doing what you're doing. I'm hearing great things." Chris would tell him.

Greg recounted a wisdom in Chris, one that he respected even though they weren't far apart in age. Chris never minced words and got right to the point. Whenever Chris spoke, Greg listened.

As he watched Chris rise through the ranks, their contact with each other fell off. While no longer logistically connected, Greg was comfortable calling Chris a friend. That's why an incident in 2015 was especially problematic.

Since the fourth grade, Greg knew his path, and while aspirations and dreams could be mighty propulsion devices, they did nothing to prepare a person for the job. A human mind and body can only take so much load, and Greg had found his stress release in his family's annual summer vacation in Old Orchard Beach, Maine. They'd sit by the fire at night, laugh until their sides split, shop the quaint stores, reminisce, and decompress. Greg considered his yearly getaway a pivotal key to his longevity in law enforcement and had raised his three children to look forward to it as much as he did.

The morning sun rising over the waves warmed Greg from the inside out. His solitary walks on the beach while his family slept in back at the house fueled a reconnection with a natural beauty so often dulled by the evil he encountered on the job. Greg always separated the brilliant colors in the sky so he could appreciate each one. How streaks of gold met pink and orange before everything gave way to an immaculate blue.

His feet sloshed through chips of broken shells buried in soft sand in a rhythmic grip and release pattern. His breathing was steady and regular, his mind serene. He greeted other walkers with a smile and a missive to have a great day. If only it could last, he thought, how grand it would be if the perfection of this place could stretch beyond the allotted dates on the calendar. He paused his walk and remained in place, gazing outward as the line of demarcation between sky and sea came into focus.

Almost lost to the illusion of a permanent seaside landscape, Greg remained connected to his surroundings in that trained trooper way. He monitored sounds, always patrolling for danger. Or, in this case, the shape of an approaching man that seemed curiously familiar.

Greg's eyes narrowed. The man got closer, his arms flat against his sides, back straight, the shadow of a baseball hat bobbing beside him as it shielded his eyes from the strengthening light.

"What's going on, man?" the man asked Greg. The voice clicked first. Greg knew that voice.

"Chris, wow. Hey, man…" He wanted his smile to remain. He tried not to let it waver, but the sight of Chris, *this Chris*, was harsh. He was unshaven, his eyes ringed by gray circles that Greg also grew when he went too long without sleep. They chatted for a few minutes and bid each other farewell, but as Chris walked away Greg remained rooted there in the sand. All those rumors and rumblings he'd been hearing about. *Major AuCoin isn't well, he's been sick.* He watched his friend until he disappeared into the distance. The unbreakable man he'd considered a machine of proficiency and expertise.

And how broken he looked now.

CHAPTER SEVENTEEN
STRAINED RELATIONS

When Chris completed his tenure as commander of the NHSP SWAT team, he offered full-throated endorsements for his successors and was proud when his guys would earn promotions within the state police. Many of them would call Chris's leadership integrally powerful in shaping their performance and capabilities. No one was more thrilled than Chris when he'd get word of a commendation, rise in rank, or new position filled by one of his own. When Mark Hall was climbing the rope to his eventual role of director of the New Hampshire Department of Safety, Division of State Police, or colonel, he still spoke with Chris often, and their families got together at the Old Orchard Beach house for summer barbecues. Those were breakthrough moments in a friendship, when Chris felt comfortable enough to let his guard down. He might've had a few beers, but nothing beyond that, and Mark considered those occasions away from work particularly dear. Being inside Chris's most inner circle felt like an honor. In that, Mark's professional reputation had been built by Chris's expectations and the mantra he insisted everyone around him adopt.

"Look like a trooper, act like a trooper," he'd repeat to them. Mark never let that waver in himself, and it became a teaching tool he later used on the new troopers who came through. "Stay fit and be mentally strong," Mark preached. He also envisioned Chris whenever he discussed the concept of putting on the armor to do the job and giving it everything you had. To wear the uniform with distinction, confidence, and pride. Just as Chris had taught him to do.

When each SWAT team member stepped away to pursue other opportunities, as Chris had, they remained close and kept in contact, mostly by phone. He and Mark spoke occasionally, but he hadn't seen his former commander in some time and detected a quake in Chris's voice when he'd called to tell Mark about his thyroid cancer diagnosis. When Mark hung up, he had to settle himself. The strongest man he had ever known, who bench pressed weights in the gym no mortal should be able to, who never complained, wavered, or let any of them down, sounded distraught. He went on with his day but closed his eyes in prayer that Chris would get through this.

Later, their paths crossed at headquarters in Concord. Mark was there on business, as was Chris, who was still doing work in his role as major. When Mark stepped from the door frame of an office and began a brisk walk down the hallway, his breath caught.

"Major?" his voice rose as if he, too, had to question if the man he saw before him was truly the same one he knew.

"Mark!"

The suit swamped him, as though Chris was a shell of himself, indented and sectioned into sunken hollows. His neck, too narrow to fill the dress shirt, the collar now so loose it gapped and draped over his skin. As they closed the distance between them, Mark held his breath again. Chris's face was an ashy gray, like a dulling filter had been laid over him and stolen away all the colors of life.

It bothered Mark for quite a while. As did the murmurings about Chris's drinking that had begun circulating within their tight-knit groups. Mark had never once seen Chris drunk, let alone out of control. He ran a tight ship with his team, but even tighter for himself. Mark wasn't sure what was happening with his mentor, only that his ship was listing and seas were running high.

—★—

Kevin Duffy felt his stomach twist when another call came in from Tracy about a month after the first one, when Chris had grabbed the phone away and hung up. *Oh, man,* he thought as he clicked the button to answer.

"Tracy, hi. What's up, everything okay?"

She told Kevin how Chris had been self-medicating with beer, and things were bad at home. How the family had tried to get him help, but nothing was sticking.

"He's coming back from McLean today," Tracy told him. "And, Kevin, I'm afraid."

The AuCoins and Tracy had managed to get Chris to McLean Hospital in Massachusetts. As Chris's behavior grew more erratic, they realized he needed an all-of-the-above approach to manage the blend of substance and psychological breadcrumbs he was leaving behind. The new anxiety he talked about with Paula, may not be simply because he was sitting behind a desk. The few beers he'd share with Brent may not be all he'd consumed that day. The expensive purchases perhaps being made to fill a hole in Chris that was growing too wide and deep for him to climb out of. The New Hampshire veteran's services programs threw down a ladder, but Chris wasn't fit to climb. Brent and Paula researched what was available, even as they couldn't pinpoint the exact diagnosis. McLean, which specialized in both addiction and psychiatric illness, seemed like a logical next step. When Chris was deemed well enough to come home again, Tracy balked. She had three daughters in the house and Chris's volatility was a risk factor. She was fearful of his anger and Kevin knew right away what he had to do. He and Chris had made a pact years ago that if anything ever happened to either of them, the other would step in and take care of the family. Kevin was doing that now without hesitation.

"Hey, Cap. I need to take a few days' leave. Got something I have to deal with." He hung up with his captain and packed a bag. He'd be away for a while.

When Kevin arrived at Chris's home in Wilton, Brent, Paula, Tracy and his daughters were all there waiting for Chris to return. His scope of what was going on with his friend was still narrow, and he listened in shock when Brent told him how bad the drinking had become. How Chris would disappear into the woods for days on end. How worried they were. How nothing was helping to get Chris better.

When Chris walked through the front door, Kevin watched his gait and eyes to gauge whether he was sober. He was. A good start. He went around the room to greet his family and then turned to Kevin.

"What are you doing here?" he demanded, not at all happy to see him.

"I'm here because I'm your friend," Kevin told him. He, too, tried to take in the physical transformation. From the gaunt face to the heavy-lidded eyes, Chris looked like he'd been through a war. When they all sat down for dinner that night, Chris was melancholy. He grunted more than spoke and moved his fork around more than ate the food on it.

"I'll take the trash out," Chris told them as everyone cleaned up. Kevin watched Chris walk out to the garage. It was tense inside the house, and he released some of the pent-up air he'd been holding while they'd tried to eat.

Minutes ticked by. Kevin checked his watch. How long had it been since Chris took out the trash?

Turns out, long enough to get himself looped. When he walked back into the house, Chris's attitude and demeanor had completely changed. Kevin wondered how this drunken person fresh out of treatment, his best friend on the job, the most upstanding man he'd ever known, could possibly be Chris.

Eventually, Kevin figured Chris must have had a stash in the garage. While he still didn't know the full spectrum of whatever it was that had been stealing Chris away, Kevin tried to assist. He worked with Tracy to coordinate doctor's visits, and he was hearing Chris say all the right things.

Yes, I want help. Yes, I need to get back to work. Yes, I'll do whatever it takes to get better.

Kevin had hope Chris would turn things around. At least until the next call came in letting him know Chris had run away from the VA in Vermont. Then, another time when he didn't have his phone and no one knew where Chris was for days. When Tracy confided she was fearful for her safety, Kevin knew she'd taken the kids and left the house for a while. Chris's circle tightened as his family and law enforcement friends tried to intervene, support, and keep his unraveling out of the public square.

But that was rapidly becoming impossible to do. Chris was accelerating toward disaster and the first of many inevitable run-ins with the law.

—★—

Police reports began to pile up from Wilton to Jaffrey, and further west to Peterborough, and they all read like a repeat episode of the same show. Chris had left his home after excessive drinking and was behind the wheel of his truck driving erratically. He couldn't complete a field sobriety test and threatened an officer. He'd been taken into protective custody, and—depending on the incident and Chris's own mood—either launched combative attacks on the responding officers, tried to induce a physical altercation, passed out, or was willing to admit he was struggling with PTSD and dealing with cancer. In May of 2015, Chris was enrolled in the Uniformed Services Program, which is a specialized mental health program for veterans, first responders, and active-duty military members experiencing a crisis. Sometimes, other members of the program would be present when Chris tried to dash away into the woods, or appeared drunk and needed to be subdued until police arrived. During one incident, he was asked by a responding officer if he was going to harm himself. Chris's response was chilling.

"If I didn't have to take care of my daughters, I would."

He was often transported to emergency departments to be medically cleared, but after several concerning incidents involving Chris's uncooperative and belligerent behavior toward medical staff, they reported no longer feeling safe treating Chris due to his level of intoxication, strength, and volatile nature. Some crisis programs wouldn't take Chris until he was sober. Many calls were made and Chris was often shuffled around to detention facilities equipped to hold him until he had slept it off. Brent and Paula awoke each day in heart-pounding fear. When the phone rang, they knew what it was about before they even answered. Chris was collapsing into a pattern of drunken debauchery, unruly and menacing conduct, and, in these worst of times, was a danger to himself and everyone around him. They were in a race to save their son and started pounding on every door they could find. And Chris's best friends were right by their side.

—★—

Chris Vetter was mowing the lawn on a Sunday morning when Kevin called.

"Hey, I need your help. We need to take a ride to Vermont. Meet me in Concord and we'll drive up together. It's really important, and it involves Chris AuCoin. I'll see you soon."

Kevin tried to prepare Vetter for what they would encounter. He told him about the drinking, the significant PTSD Chris was experiencing, the efforts to salvage his career. His life and family. How he'd take off into the woods for a couple days to disappear. The sneaking around and hiding alcohol.

"You're going to see him and he's different from anything you've ever seen of him before," Kevin explained. "I need you to be prepared for what this looks like."

Vetter sat in the truck, often too stunned to speak. He listened to Kevin brief him about Chris's bouts of heavy intoxication, clashes with local police, arrests, the loss of his drivers' license, trouble with his wife, and family. The ride to the VA in White River Junction, Vermont was taut with heavy thoughts. Kevin already knew what this decline looked like up close, but Vetter was running possibilities through his own mind—visions of a Chris he might not recognize. Unruly and threatening? Drunk and disorderly? As the miles ticked by, he was highly conflicted about what he was about to step into. About laying eyes on a man he considered to be the most emotionally regulated person he'd ever known. He tried to remember the last conversation with Chris. While he'd known about the medical hit he'd endured, Vetter had no clue about the rest of it.

"He never let on that anything was wrong," Vetter said quietly, lost in the awfulness of this shocking reality.

"No one knows it's this bad," Kevin told him. "And we keep this tight. Just you and me. No one else. We tell no one else." They would protect Chris like the brother he was.

The VA medical campus in Vermont sat beneath low mountain peaks and bundles of pine trees. They pulled in and began the walk into the building where Chris was being held inside. While Kevin had tried to warn Vetter that it would be difficult to see, when they entered the room where Chris was, the sight of him took his breath away. Laid out on a hospital bed, wearing a johnnie, drunk, and very angry, he let Vetter have it the minute he saw him step around the curtain.

"What the hell are you doing here?" he hurled. "Get the hell out of here, man!"

Chris screamed at Vetter to leave for several minutes. He thrashed and rolled, his teeth gnashed together and his face bright red. Finally, when Chris had burned himself out, Vetter told him why he was there.

"Look, Chris," he began, "I'll go wait in the lobby, but if there's anything I've learned from you, it's that you would never leave one of your guys behind. So, I'll go sit, but I'm not leaving you when you're in trouble."

Chris's eyes tracked Vetter and held, his face going from menacing to chagrined, and then back to rage filled. The cycle was exhausting and devastating. Vetter took a seat in the room as Chris spoke mostly to Kevin. Occasionally, he'd throw Vetter a disturbed sneer but allowed him to stay. Doctors came and went, but time was the largest participant in the process. Chris's system had to metabolize the alcohol before any further work or analysis of his condition could be done. Many hours passed with Vetter and Kevin in the room. Chris would hover between worlds, awake yet guarded, then asleep and still. As he sobered up, he repeated lines he knew his friends preferred to hear: *I'll work on it, it's not that bad, I'm okay, really.* While Vetter's instinct was to believe this was just a one-off, an isolated spin Chris would pull out of, Kevin had seen enough to have little faith that was the course they were all about to follow.

—★—

"Kevin, it's Tracy. Chris ran away from the VA in Brattleboro. We don't know where he is, he doesn't have his phone."

Kevin swore under his breath. Out on a detail, he had no choice but to try and find his friend. He clicked on Chris Vetter's number and called.

"Be ready in fifteen. I'm coming to get you." Kevin hung up the phone. He knew Vetter was in the middle of SWAT training, yet he needed him. Chris needed them both. An incoming text told him Chris had just been found but he was being held in the ER section of the VA facility until he detoxed. Typically, those were the hours when Chris was at his worst.

Vetter spent the ride trying to figure out what he'd say when they arrived. Kevin was stewing in his own thoughts. The rate of incidents was rising, and Chris was becoming dangerously volatile given his size, durability, and superior survival skills. Getting Chris contained was like facing down a charging bear as it made quick work of closing the distance. Limited time to think before the full brunt of it arrived right in your face.

"He'll probably still be drunk," Kevin said.

"Got it."

"He'll be angry."

"Yes."

When they arrived, Chris was in a rage. Eyes wild, drunken slurs and hollered threats bounced off the walls in ricocheted waves of clunky clatter. As Kevin and Vetter entered, Chris saw them and erupted.

"Get the hell out!"

"Come on, man, you need to calm down."

"Get out!" Chris screamed again, his face pinched in agony. "Get out!"

"No, man, we're here to help. But you gotta chill, you gotta sit and calm down."

Chris yelled and hollered. His arms flailed around and his legs kicked out. Kevin and Vetter looked at each other; sadness darkened their eyes. Now, both had a full understanding that what had made Chris the best trooper and SWAT commander they'd ever known also made him the worst drunk. The stubbornness that kept his team protected on the job now meant he wouldn't listen to anyone's advice. The strong convictions that made him confident in moment-to-moment situations, now tricked his ego into thinking he knew exactly what he was doing, so screw anyone who objected.

Vetter and Kevin stayed by Chris's side in that dank holding cell all night, breathing in the stench of stale booze, cleaning solutions, and whatever muck had been dragged in on shoes and pantlegs. Chris's furious haze broke sometime during the night, and he looked more like himself again.

His friends took it for what it was, which was very likely just temporary. A dreadful truth was acknowledged on the ride back to New Hampshire.

Neither Kevin nor Vetter could predict with any certainty how this would end.

CHAPTER EIGHTEEN
BUDDY

Nate became accustomed to his phone pinging at all hours. When his parents couldn't find Chris, or he'd been arrested again and Nate had to go collect him from jail. Or, when Chris's daughters would alert him that Chris was drinking again and the temperature inside the house was rising, they were scared for Tracy. Nate would arrive, speak to Chris in some way only the two of them understood, and leave again once he'd passed out. It went like that so often he'd learned to expect an interruption at any time. One night in May of 2015, it was one of Chris's daughters on the phone.

"He's not here, Uncle Nate. We don't know where he is. But we're getting worried."

Brent and Paula were away at the Florida house, and Nate declined to alert them of the call as he got dressed and hurried out of his home in Rindge. He ticked through the possible locations where Chris could be hiding and started at the most logical one: their parents' house in Jaffrey. When tensions rose at home, Chris often stayed with Brent and Paula, and he knew the house was empty that month. Nate's mind raced through recent incidents with Chris, and how his brother seemed to have only two speeds, either drunk and furious, or completely blank. He thought of yet another recent intervention, with Chris drunk in a hotel room in Nashua, a Market Basket grocery bag by his side stuffed with thirty different prescription bottles.

"Here's half the problem!" Nate had declared. "All this in your system, plus a case of beer, what do you expect?"

He rubbed his tired eyes and remembered loading Chris into his vehicle and dropping him off at another rehab. Maybe he'd been good for a month after that stint, maybe less. All Nate knew was that night, Chris wasn't okay and he had to find him.

His parents' house appeared in the distance. Nate pulled closer, noticing the main driveway that arched around the house was empty. He squinted toward the lake. There it was. Chris's truck, parked in the dirt path that led to the water's edge, hidden by foliage unless you were specifically looking for it. Nate's fingers tightened on the wheel, and his breath quickened. Why was Chris's truck near the water, and where was Chris?

The lights were on in the house. Nate's brain wasn't yet connecting Chris's truck oddly parked nearby but as he placed his hand on the doorknob, it hit like a bolt to his heart. He'd heard a humming. An engine running. Chris's truck! Why was Chris's truck, down near the lake, running?

He broke out in a sprint across the yard, his feet pounding a path down to the truck, realizing this could be intentional. His brother had parked his truck, left it running, and it was possibly all done on purpose.

"Chris!" he screamed, hearing his brother's name tear from his throat. "Chris!"

The truck vibrated. Nate raced around the cab toward the truck's rear and saw it then; a rag stuffed into the tailpipe and a hose that ran from it and into the open crack of a window. He hit the truck, feeling the metal connecting with the skin on his knuckles and open palms.

"Chris!" he screeched out his brother's name repeatedly, and then wrapped his fingers around the handle, tugging the door open. The wild look on Chris's face told Nate he'd interrupted him, and he was furious about that in the way a starving animal would be if a slab of meat was ripped from its jaws.

"No, man. No, no, you can't do this. Chris, you can't do this!"

Nate's body braced for Chris's violent counter, because he was always a fighter, and Nate was messing with his process. He tucked his chin into his chest and planted his feet to absorb the massive assault. He went into middle brother mode, focusing on all the missives he'd learned would work on Chris in his drunkenness and psychosis—*that they had to stick together, that no one knew them like the other, that he couldn't do this to his family, that everyone needed him.* Nate kept the intentional chatter going for almost an hour by the running truck as Chris spoke of things so disturbing Nate choked back sobs. His brother's mind had been lost, pulverized into bizarre and macabre delusions of the devil; the wickedness of Satan that had seeped into his reality as he battled with the Christian values he'd lived by for his entire life. Nate saw it clearly as a war between the savagery of evil and the lightness of good. His brother was metaphorically caught on the razor's edge that ran between both.

"Come on, buddy, it's cold out here. Let's get in the house and talk there."

When Chris was within the grips of an episode, Nate called him *buddy* to de-escalate and remind him they were forever friends. Whenever it was a brawl and fists were flying, he was always *Chris.* He continued to speak softly to his brother as he led him toward the front door and over the threshold. Chris was almost folded in half, entirely exhausted and temporarily pliable to his brother's coaxing.

"Good job, buddy, come on in. Let's just sit for a minute."

Nate took a seat at the kitchen table, raked his hands over his face and shuffled through his options. Chris needed help. The hose into the truck elevated this to a level Nate could no longer manage. Even though the family knew the risks of reporting this to local police, Nate didn't see another way around it.

"Hold tight, buddy. I'll be right back. Just sit here, please, and wait for me to come back. Okay, buddy? You got me?"

Chris responded, but there was no life in his eyes. As Nate closed the door and drove over to the Jaffrey police department, he prayed for an answer to this woeful dilemma. He needed help to get Chris into the intensive treatment he needed. He also had a job expecting him to show up in the morning and had to be present and intact for his own family and children who always took the brunt when he had to race out to deal with Chris. He juggled the weight of all that plus the hellish vision of the hose in the truck that he couldn't clear from his mind. Then there was the holding of a delicate balance between rock bottom and maintaining enough good grace with the NHSP to ensure Chris could retire with his full complement of benefits. Every incident, scuffle, arrest, call for help, and report that Chris was out of control risked that.

At the police department, Nate was met by two officers who knew him, his family, and Chris's instability. He told them what he'd discovered down by the lake and that he believed it was an intentional effort by Chris to take his own life.

"I need to get him somewhere. Maybe take him into protective custody, please, I have to work tomorrow, I can't do this all night. My family's worried about me. We're all worried about Chris. I don't know what to do, but Chris needs help."

The police would eventually respond to the house, but not until things took a violently dangerous turn.

—★—

Nate's legs moved like they were leaden trunks as he left his truck and walked back toward the front door of his parents' home. His anguish tilted back to alarm when he heard synthesized and atmospheric music blaring from inside. Chris had loaded Enya into the speakers and turned the volume to full blast. He swung his eyes around the kitchen. The living room. He had to find Chris!

"Chris! Where are you? Turn that down!"

He looked in every room and around every corner. His brother, the quintessential expert at disappearing himself, becoming unseen somehow, had tucked himself into one of the last rooms Nate searched. His breath released on a flutter of hot air; Chris resembled that wary, cornered animal again—his eyes shuttered and blank.

"Turn that down, Chris. Let's go sit and talk. Come on, let's go." And then Nate, himself a heavy drinker for decades, went for the sure thing. The one thing Chris would agree to do. "Let's have a couple of drinks."

In retrospect, Nate would call that invitation a product of his own idiocy but that was the path he sought. To get Chris so drunk he'd pass out and sleep it off so Nate could leave. He'd return to check on him in the morning, when Chris was sober.

The ethereal notes of music quelled, but Chris's mood roiled. He'd worked his madness into an unrequited neurosis, so consumed by disease and bitterness he couldn't see Nate as anything other than an adversary. An enemy that needed to be put down.

"Get out," he told him.

"No, Chris, let's get a drink. Let's just sit."

Chris's muscles tensed. His eyes slitted into darkness. "Nate, leave now."

"No, man. I'm not leaving."

He rushed him. Chris heaved himself into Nate's chest, knocking him into a lamp that tumbled to the floor as the coffee table it stood upon quaked. Nate heard wood snapping and the swoosh of air exiting his lungs. Instinctively, he threw his arms up to protect his face and head. Chris was an unstoppable battering ram, coming for Nate's most vulnerable commodity, the very air he needed to live.

"Chris, stop! Stop!" he choked. They rolled over furniture and slammed against walls. Pictures of the three brothers crashed to the ground, their glass frames smashing even as their smiles from happier times remained frozen. Nate could hear his own exertion, his stilted breath and pained groans, but it was what he could see that sickened him most.

"Chris! Stop!"

Heavier than Nate and trained to disable and destroy, Chris was swept up in adrenaline and that heightened state of physical alertness and invincible power. He bounced on the balls of his feet to intercept Nate's attempts to get around him, eventually pinning him between the wall and a couch. "Chris, stop!" He screamed into the abyss as Chris stalked and cornered him, threw him onto his back, and wrapped his fingers around Nate's neck. With the full weight of Chris on his chest and the tightening grip on his neck, Nate couldn't breathe. He counted off seconds.

Ten seconds.

His fingernails ripped into Chris's skin as he tried to claw his hands away.

Fifteen seconds.

Chris's eyes bulged, his face red and hot like lava was pumping through his veins, his teeth bared. Feral. The presumed victor in a death match.

Twenty seconds.

Nate knew he had about ten seconds left before the oxygen deprivation and pressure on his windpipe stopped his heart.

"Buddy," he growled, his voice a tortured garble.

Twenty-five seconds.

"Buddy. Buddy. Buddy." His code word. The one Nate always used on Chris to bring him back. To remind him they were brothers. Family. Forever connected.

The urge to close his eyes was unbearable. "Bud—"

The veil lifted. Chris's eyes blinked clear again and his fingers let go. Nate rolled onto his side and grabbed for air, trying to deliver it straight into his lungs like cooling water being poured over crispy and dehydrated sand. Chris sat back on his heels. When Nate could face him again Chris's expression was one of complete consternation. As though his heart was asking his soul how he could have almost killed his own brother. His buddy.

"It's okay," Nate squeaked. "We're okay. This is no problem at all, Chris."

Chris helped Nate stand and together they went outside.

"We have to figure this out," Nate told him. He did not speak of the brawl. The truck. He just knew above all else he had to keep Chris calm.

That worked for about fifteen minutes. Then, as though a simmering ember inside him caught fresh wind, Chris exploded anew. He punched the siding on the house. Squared himself. Punched it again. And again.

"No, no, no!" Nate yelled. "No, Chris, we have to stay calm and figure this out. Come on!"

Chris faced him, his eyes turning again. Darkening.

"Why am I doing this?" he hissed at Nate. "What is happening to me?"

Chris pleaded for answers that Nate couldn't provide. He could only listen and support. "I don't know, Chris. We have to figure it out."

He railed against life, God, and the longing inside of himself for how he used to be. For the man he was. "Why do I feel like this, Nate? Why?"

Nate stepped toward Chris but then held himself in place. He sensed another shift. Chris was elevating back into that seething fever state that preferred violence and brutality. Chris turned back to the wall of the house and unleashed a rapid series of punches.

"Chris, stop!" Nate made a whiplash choice to intervene, to save Chris and the house from further damage. He grabbed his brother's midsection and pulled him back from the indents in the siding where Chris's fists had landed. "Stop!"

Chris's eyes went blank again, hardened by the poison of his misdirected hatred. He pushed Nate's arms away and then shoved him hard. Nate stumbled backward, nearly tripped, already fearing the imminent return of Chris's fingers back around his neck, squeezing his life away for good this time. Chris pounced on him and kept coming like a machine programmed to incapacitate.

Nate had milliseconds to protect himself. He twisted his back toward Chris and then pushed at him to build space. He saw a gallon of paint on a bench next to the house. He stretched his fingers out, trying to grasp the thin metal loop at the top. It slipped. He stretched again until he felt the handle. He looped it beneath his fingers and dropped his shoulders. His elbow bent with the weight of the steel can as it traveled in an arc, down and then up, with as much force as Nate could manage.

The paint can struck the back of Chris's head with a dense plunk and tore open a gash that trickled out a river of blood onto Chris's shirt and the ground outside of their parents' home. Nate could hear Chris's lungs losing air, a last gasp before his consciousness slipped away and he hit the ground with a thud.

Nate put his elbows on his knees and steadied his breathing. He bent down and managed to haul Chris up and then turned him over onto his back. His eyes were closed, mouth gaped open. Nate fumbled through his pocket. Found his phone. Dialed 9-1-1.

"I got into a fight," he told dispatch. "My brother's bleeding from the head. We need an ambulance." So much for avoiding another police report, he thought, and figured it was about to get even uglier for his family.

As for the police report itself, the event was detailed in a way that put fault on both brothers. That by the time officers responded to the AuCoin home, Chris was standing on the lawn wrapped in a towel. According to the report, Nate told officers, with spilled paint all over his legs, that to get Chris off him he'd struck him with the paint can.

"You're under arrest for assault," the officer told Chris, placed him in handcuffs, then checked them for fit and to ensure they were double locked. He, too, was covered in paint. As Chris was being loaded into the cruiser, Nate was stricken by grief and sadness.

"I love you, buddy," he called to his brother.

"I love you, too, Nate." Chris responded. "Don't worry about this."

Chris was taken to the police station where they were met by an ambulance for evaluation.

"My head hurts," Chris told them. He requested medical attention and mentioned the mistake the officers were making for not arresting his brother, too. Multiple times the report describes the strong stench of alcohol wafting off both Chris and Nate. With Chris in the booking room, medical attendants arrived and began to treat him until he passed out and stopped responding to stimulus. From there, Chris was put on a stretcher and transported to the hospital where he received several staples to close the cut on the back of his head. When consciousness returned, Chris told officers many times he did not wish to press charges against Nate, and that he should be released. He also tore at the heart monitor leads and blood pressure cuff to leave. He flailed and fumbled around the bed for some time, but eventually, Chris broke down and the pain rushed out of him in the way a wracking truth tended to.

"I have PTSD from my time in the military," he admitted to the officer while they were together in the ER. "And from SWAT. I've also been battling cancer." With bloodshot eyes and a crushed spirit, Chris spoke of what he knew was happening, even though he could never tell his family all the secrets he divulged while in the care of a police officer and emergency room doctor. He simply could never let them think he was anything other than indestructible, even as his illness was laid bare by his actions, drinking, and explosiveness, and his life had fallen into shambles.

The ER doctor put together a plan to keep Chris for observation and ordered a mental health evaluation for the morning. Chris agreed. Then two of his most trusted friends pulled back the curtain of the ER triage room he was being held in and reinforced what needed to happen.

—★—

Sean Haggerty felt his shoulders sag as Tracy told him over the phone that Chris and Nate had gotten into a fight and Chris was at the hospital.

"I'm on my way," he told her. He then texted his other friend and told him to get ready to go, that Chris was in trouble and needed them.

Sean and another member of Chris's SWAT team under his command took in the sight of him, laid out on a hospital bed and in a johnnie, yet his legs were covered in hardened, stuck on paint.

"Got yourself into something pretty good, Chris, didn't you." They started.

"Yeah," he told them. "Fight with Nate and a paint can. Obviously."

They knew of Chris's situation. Sean had scooped him up from a bar several times to drive him safely home, but this version of Chris was jarring and it shook Sean. They settled into the small examination room and stayed for hours.

"I messed up," Chris would say.

"Sure, but it's all fixable," they'd tell him.

"No, man. This is bad. This time it's bad."

Chris was sobering up and realizing the far-reaching implications of his actions.

"We're going to take you back to Vermont," Sean told him.

"No…" Chris started to object but stopped himself. Sean sensed an opening.

"It's the best thing right now, Chris. It's what you need. They can help you."

Chris's eyes turned sharp. "No one can help me."

"What? No, Chris. That's not true at all. When we get you back to Vermont, they'll get you settled back in. They can help you get better."

Chris looked directly at Sean. "I screwed this up," he said, his face so bleak and hopeless Sean felt his throat go raw. He swallowed before he spoke again.

"Chris, this is fixable. We'll get you back there and you'll fix all of it."

Eventually, Chris was released to Sean and his former SWAT team member who drove him back to the VA in Vermont, walked him into the lobby, and told him everything would be okay.

As they drove back home to New Hampshire, they fervently hoped they were right.

—★—

Back at the AuCoin house, Nate was also arrested though all charges were eventually reduced to misdemeanors or dropped. However, in that small town way, news of the brothers' skirmish was absorbed along with that morning's first load of coffee. Tongues wagged and clucked, heads shook in sadness, and for Nate, the burden of that incident was life-altering. His kids were young at the time, and when their friends' parents saw news reports about the fight, his arrest, the drinking, and the chaos, they kept their children away. Nate's family, yet again, caught in the bands of a spinning hurricane; a raging storm that both broke his heart and infuriated him.

How do I tell them I was trying to save my brother? Nate couldn't imagine anyone understanding that. That it was an arduous battle he'd waged to make sure Chris didn't kill himself that night.

Nate saw Chris a week or two later once he was released from the VA in Vermont and back home with Tracy and the girls. They went for a walk, just the two of them.

"Oh, hey, look." Chris turned his head to show Nate the four-inch-long scar in the shape of a paint can bottom. "You got me good, you fucker."

The bond between the brothers could bend and stretch. They could argue and fight, bleed even, and then come back together again. But Nate was getting weary, and the inevitability of the next phone call was like living in a pressure cooker.

When there was a problem, Nate would show up. But during the times there wasn't a problem, he felt that Chris was nonexistent. While Chris had swaths of weeks when he wasn't explosive, manic or aggressive, Nate saw it not as calm but as numb.

He'd come by to say hello, have some coffee with his brother, but then watch Chris sitting in his chair, lifeless. He'd try to talk about something but there was no life in Chris. Except for the gym, his place of peace, which Chris always wanted to escape to, Nate watched him slip away.

Chris called Nate from time to time and asked if he wanted to join him on a hike or take the boat out to do some fishing. Nate would tell him, *sure, that sounded great* even as he had no intention of showing up. When another call came in and Chris was in trouble again, Nate would arrive, talk him down, get him back into a treatment center.

"Come on, buddy, let's figure this out."

But no one seemed to know how. Nate watched his parents age before his eyes, their pain unbearable and so deep it was cellular. As though their very DNA was changing under the stress and strain. Talking to them about it was impossible.

"Dad, enough is enough. You look so old. Stop doing this! Chris is going to kill you!" He'd beg Brent to end the cycle, even though he knew his parents couldn't possibly. Unconditional love is never that simple.

"Nate, I can't stop." Brent would tell him, his voice bleak yet forever determined.

"You're my father, too! My kids are your grandkids! If you're dead, they have nothing."

The months passed into years. Nate grew a business and focused on his family. Logic told him he had to protect his own wife and children, and after years of answering the calls that came in at all hours, Nate finally stopped.

"I'm not doing this anymore," he told Brent. "I'm done, Dad."

On that terrible December night in 2022, it was Chris who called Nate. It was late. Nate's blood chilled when he heard his brother's voice.

"Hey, where are you, Chris?"

"Never mind that."

"You okay, buddy?"

"Yup. Hey, Nate?"

"Yeah?"

"I want you to know that I love you, and if I ever hurt you or do anything to hurt you, I love you and I'm sorry."

"Where are you, buddy? Let me come see you."

"No. See you soon, Nate."

As Chris ended the call, Nate imagined the good man he'd always been. As straight and committed as anyone could ever be, caring, kind, and exceptionally strong. He closed his eyes as the image of his big brother's face filled his mind.

CHAPTER NINETEEN
FLORIDA

Later in 2015, the decision for Chris to retire from his position as major of the New Hampshire State Police was finalized. While he had some good months when the drinking stopped and he was more clear-headed, the state made it known he was no longer considered viable to hold any position in law enforcement. With his retirement in hand, benefits secured, Chris left the only job he'd ever known.

And immediately got worse.

"I feel as though Chris is losing his sense of purpose," Brent told Paula. They came to realize their son's battle had erupted into something they never could have imagined.

And that was saying something, given what the AuCoin family had already endured.

—★—

On October 11th that year, Brent and Paula delivered Chris to Talbott Recovery Center in Atlanta, Georgia. They'd researched programs and in-patient availability up and down the east coast and decided Talbott's exceptional reputation for addiction and mental health treatment was

Chris's next best option. Given the complexity of his PTSD, health problems, addictions, and temper, the notion of long-term recovery became a slippery goal. Chris had good weeks, a string of solid months, but when he lurched out of line, it was clear how fragile and precarious his survival had become. Every move they made was to save his life, but Chris wasn't always willing to go along with their plans.

He returned to New Hampshire for Christmas, and exhibited significant signs of depression, fatigue, and anxiety. Brent and Paula noted twitchiness, irritability, and a lack of focus in Chris, even as he spent time with his family and them. As the calendar turned to a new year, Chris was due back in Atlanta to complete his program at Talbott. He arrived and checked in but didn't stay long.

For unknown reasons, Chris left Talbott, rented a car, and headed for his parents' townhouse in Vero Beach. That coincided with Brent and Paula's planned trip to Florida, but Chris refused to answer their calls and by the time they arrived at the townhouse, he'd disappeared.

"Please, can you please help us?" they begged the desk attendant at the Quality Inn about a mile from their townhouse on Route 1. Once they put the pieces together that Chris was driving a rental car, not answering his phone, and likely having an episode, Brent and Paula scoured the strip, searching hotel parking lots and lobbies. The Quality Inn was a hit, and the attendant was empathetic to their plight. He agreed to look up Chris's name and confirmed he was staying in one of their units.

The door to that unit was cracked open and dark inside.

"Chris?" Brent called. He tapped his knuckles against the door. "Chris?"

They didn't want to startle or alarm Chris with loud banging or strained voices given how unpredictable he'd become.

"Chris?" Paula tentatively ventured through the door crack when he didn't answer. They gently pushed it open and entered. Paula placed her hand over her heart as a rush of despair stole her breath. Brent raced over to the bed where Chris was laid out, motionless and still.

The stench was powerful, a mustiness masked by old food and alcohol.

"Oh, no," Brent whispered, his eyes scanning the room. Dried-up pizza slices sat in their oil-stained square box, and empty beer cans, dozens of them, had tumbled from the nightstand onto the discolored and frayed rug. "Oh, Chris."

Paula walked toward the dresser. "Brent, over here." She pointed to two empty vodka bottles. Chris had downed an incredible amount of alcohol and wasn't responding to Brent's nudges.

"Chris, wake up." He pushed on Chris's shoulder. "Wake up."

The disarray of the room, the horrid smell of waste and alcoholism, shattered them. The brittle hope they'd had that this time and place would pull their son back to them, fractured.

"We have to get him up," Paula said, her voice straining. "Wake him up."

"I'm trying," Brent told her. "He's out cold."

They flanked Chris on the bed. Paula on one side, Brent on the other. They pushed his shoulders, tried to shake his hands, rattled and patted his cheeks and head. It took some time, but Chris finally opened his eyes, saw them there, and became entirely uncooperative.

"We're leaving, Chris. Come on, get yourself together. You need some help." They begged him as they'd had to before. To help them save him. To get him back to Tracy and the girls. Back to New Hampshire, the gym, his friends. "Please, come with us."

"No," Chris told them. "No, I can't do this. I can't."

Daylight was fading when Chris finally agreed to let his parents take him to the VA in West Palm. During the drive, they'd stopped at another facility, one that offered in-patient treatment and had been known to transform even the most challenging cases. Chris took a few steps across the parking lot of The Horizon Recovery Center and froze.

"Oh, no, no, no."

"Chris, please, let's just get inside. We can talk to someone. Let's just get you through the front door."

Paula followed Chris's stony stare and turned her head to see what had caused him to falter. She sighed in defeat when she saw the iron bars on the windows. She turned toward Brent, who noticed them at the same time.

"I can't. I won't. I can't be locked in. Please, Mom, please, Dad, if this is a locked facility, I am not staying!"

He remained where he was as Brent and Paula reached the main entrance and rang a bell on the door to enter the facility. But it was short-lived once an employee confirmed the facility was exactly that, to protect them and their patients from violence and injury. They required a lock-down period for detox.

"Forget it!" Chris stormed off and they continued the drive to the VA.

Inside the VA's emergency department, Chris was agitated and impatient, hostile and rude to the staff. A side of him his parents had never seen. The irony was when he was finally admitted, it was to the hospital's fourth floor, a lockdown unit for its detox program. Chris ended up in exactly what he had refused and had to stay there for three days. By mid-January, Chris was attending AA meetings and opening up to the group about his challenges. Many members flocked to Chris to tell him that his honesty and willingness to be vulnerable would be transformational in this battle. They knew his sickness because it was theirs, too.

—★—

Brent and Paula were so encouraged by Chris's commitment to AA and the new supportive relationships he was building, they felt comfortable enough to return to New Hampshire. By late January, they were racing back down to Florida again.

"Chris is calling me," Tracy told them. "He's telling me he wants to end his life."

Brent called the sheriff's office in Florida, explained what was going on with Chris, and requested a welfare check. Given he'd left their townhouse again, they were able to confirm he'd checked back in at the same Quality Inn where they'd first found him earlier that month. When the sheriff's department arrived, they found Chris, who had relapsed in another astounding display of alcoholic gluttony, and then transported him to a nearby hospital where he was admitted. The AuCoins boarded another plane and landed back in Florida, which felt ominous, given what they knew they were there to do.

With the help of a court order, Chris was remanded to the hospital for an involuntary assessment and stabilization process, which meant he no longer had the legal free will to check himself out. As his parents stood outside the hospital, unsure if they should enter, who they needed to contact, or if they should be there, Chris called Brent's cell phone. Paula had decided to leave Chris's medication with the staff, and as she returned, Chris was screaming so loudly she could hear him as Brent held the phone away from his ear.

"Dad! Dad, get me out of here!" he begged.

"Chris, we can't do that," Brent explained, trying to keep his voice level. "You have to stay here for a while. The doctors won't let you leave. We can't get you out right now. You need help."

"Dad!" Chris laid down insults and pleas, his nastiness rising with a furious realization that he was not the one calling the shots. "Dad, be a man and get your wife under control!" he roared at Brent and then ended the call.

Two days later, Chris was released into the care of his parents, who listened with tears streaming down their cheeks to his remorseful apologies. They forgave him as they always did. When he went back to AA and rejoined the group there, Paula stayed with Chris in Florida while Brent returned to New Hampshire. He was all right for a while, but the pressure behind the overly burdened dam holding him together was causing it to strain and buckle. On March 1st, Paula reluctantly returned to New Hampshire, but she had that bad feeling.

By March 4th, the sheriff's department made two more welfare checks on Chris and determined he had relapsed, but there was nothing more they could do.

On March 7th, Brent and Paula flew back to Florida. It was early morning and Chris was asleep in the upstairs bedroom at their townhouse. He was hung over, outraged to see his parents there, and refused to go anywhere with them or accept help.

"Leave me alone!" he screamed at them. "I don't need your help and I don't want it!"

They pleaded like they always did, hoping for that sliver of agreeability to reopen in Chris so they could maneuver him peacefully to the car and find another center, hospital, VA, or doctor who could reach him. But this time, Chris wasn't having it.

"Fine," he told them. "If you won't leave, then I will."

And he did. He left without telling him where he intended to go or what he would do.

"What now?" Paula asked, shaky and scared. "How do we do this?"

Brent could only shake his head, because he had no clue.

***

When their phone rang later that day, another Florida police officer was on the other end.

"I'm calling about Christopher AuCoin," he told them.

Their stomachs seized. So many of these calls and they still felt that unbridled uneasiness.

"He's our son, yes."

"Well, we got a report about a man passed out in his car in front of a store."

Brent put his hand to his face. The officer explained this had happened in downtown Vero, and that he'd found two bottles of vodka on the front seat of Chris's car.

"Thing is, I can't do anything because the car keys were in the trunk."

"Can we take him to the VA in West Palm Beach?" Brent asked.

"You can try, sir, but I'm not sure how far you'll get."

Turns out, they got nowhere. Chris refused to go with them, but eventually they learned a friend from AA, also a former Marine, had managed to get Chris back to the hospital where he was held for five days. During that time, the AuCoins resorted back to the law to initiate The Baker Act, which in Florida allowed for the involuntary hold of a person deemed to be a danger to himself or others and likely to neglect his own well-being. It also would cover them when Chris inevitably tried to check himself back out of the hospital. They wouldn't need it however, because during that hospitalization, Chris met a nurse who spoke freely about her faith in God and His saving grace.

"I feel like this nurse has been sent to me," he told his parents. "Sent to me by God. I think this time will be different."

He asked them not to pursue the legal hold and agreed to a treatment plan. The judge dropped their request, and The Baker Act option was eliminated. For now.

Paula stayed with Chris in Florida as he attended private therapy for alcohol abuse and trauma. He increased the number of visits he made to the VA within the substance abuse and PTSD program and committed to daily AA meetings and family counseling sessions. He also set up times to volunteer so his mind was engaged and his appetite to self-destruct eased. They talked about reuniting with Tracy and his girls back in New Hampshire, and Chris was working his way toward defined goals to get him home again.

For the first five weeks, everything went exactly as planned.

By April, with Paula back in New Hampshire, Chris got quiet. Calls went unanswered, and he lost contact with his parents again. On April 12th, officers returned to the AuCoin's Florida townhouse twice to perform welfare checks on Chris, who had been drunk, called Tracy, and threatened to harm himself. With their hands tied yet again, the officers relented to Chris's explanation that he was, in fact, fine, and left him alone. When a friend from AA arrived the next morning to try again to save Chris's life, he came out to his car wrapped in a towel, holding his wallet and phone. Paula booked another ticket to Florida and arrived back at the townhouse the next day.

And what she found inside was dreadful.

CHAPTER TWENTY
A RESPECT

Beer cans mingled with dried wine splotches and vodka bottles on tables and counters. The air was stale and thick with sourness. Paula walked a narrow path toward the kitchen, stepping over debris strewn across the floor. She swung open the fridge and peered inside. A lone container of American chop suey sat on an otherwise empty shelf. The townhouse was muted and dark as Paula climbed the stairs to the second floor where the bedrooms were. She was disquieted by what she'd discovered already but Chris's bedroom revealed far worse.

She caught her breath as her hand rose to cover her mouth. She saw something familiar in the middle of the bed, recognizing the Marine emblem on the top of a wooden box one of Chris's girls had given him as a gift. She walked to the bed and gently lifted the lid. Inside the box were treasures from her son's life: pictures of their family at his USMC graduation weekend in Parris Island, of his daughters, and his grandfather. She moved her fingers softly around several sentimental trinkets and paused to allow her skin to feel the beads on a rosary he'd placed inside. Misery washed over her as she analyzed her own face in the picture with Brent and the boys. Of course, she'd been worried about what Chris would see and do overseas, but the pride she'd felt in the young man they'd raised was what she could remember shining the brightest that day. The selfless ambition Chris had to serve and protect the innocent of his nation, and then his town, community, and state. Memories flew through her head. Chris as a young man. His eyes so clear and intentional, his childhood love for a pony named Fern, his temperament and calm stoicism guiding him to make impossible decisions that his gut told him were proper and necessary. His work ethic and love for the sea. A steep rise through the ranks of the state police. The SWAT team he'd led through danger and crisis. The family he'd built. How had it all slipped away? How and when had their rock begun to break? Hypothetical questions churned in her mind as she sat on the corner of the bed and tucked all the pictures, rosary, and other items back into Chris's box.

Paula had always been able to gather herself back together after an upsetting event, but this, with Chris, had manifested into something so formidable and terrifying she felt lost in the magnitude of its largeness. She allowed herself a few more minutes in the quiet of the bedroom, with Chris's items nearby, to calm her heart rate and focus her purpose.

Her one job as a mother was to protect her children, even when they were grown and making whiplash decisions that could destroy their lives. With that, she stood up, went downstairs, and shuffled back through what needed to happen next. Chris was in the hospital detoxing again. She had to make sure he stayed there. Legal action to involuntarily hold Chris was already in progress once again, giving her a few more days before his stabilization would be reexamined and his release was imminent. As history would indicate, that's when Chris tended to be his angriest. She refiled a petition to enact the Baker Act to hold Chris another 72 hours, but there was a risk his current hold would expire before a judge could approve her request. She also reached out to the AA friend who had brought Chris back to the hospital and arranged for him to move Chris's car, so it was no longer available to him when he came back to the townhouse.

Then, she waited for the inevitable explosion that would follow.

When Chris learned what she had done.

—★—

"Mom! Where are you? Where's my car? I'm at the townhouse and I can't get in!"

Sure enough, Chris was released just before the judge granted Paula's petition to hold him. Enraged after walking five miles from the hospital to the townhouse only to realize his car was gone and he was locked out, Chris peppered his mother's phone with call after call. The messages he left for her grew increasingly threatening.

"Mom, pick up."

And then, "Mom, you'd better pick up. Trust me, you'd better talk to me!"

Paula had to buy time. It gutted her not to answer Chris's calls, but she couldn't let on she was working legal channels to keep him in detox for a few more days. They had to find an alternative to Chris being released only to relapse within hours or days. The moment she received notification the court had approved her petition, she obtained a copy and hand-delivered it to the county sheriff's office. A deputy introduced himself.

"Hello, I'm Chris."

Paula's mouth tugged into a tiny and melancholy twitch. The deputy named Chris led her to a small conference room and sat down to listen. She poured out the peril of what their lives had become, who Chris had been, and the extraordinary life he'd had before trauma, stress, PTSD, and alcoholism had ruptured it. Deputy Chris took notes and asked questions, and all the while her Chris called and called. In the lividness of one of his more strenuous voicemails, he also dropped a clue about his location. It was all Deputy Chris would need to help Paula attain those few extra days to plan their next steps. He rolled out in the direction of a Chili's restaurant.

—★—

Without keys, a car, and his mother not picking up his calls, Chris walked from the townhouse to the Chili's, settled himself on a barstool and ordered a burger and a beer. His position gave him an unobstructed view of the parking lot, so when he saw police cruisers park outside, Chris left the Chili's and went to stand before the officers outside. Deputy Chris then met Chris AuCoin face to face, while backup officers lined up behind them.

"Not sure what you're doing here, but I'm not going anywhere with you," Chris told them, defiant and confrontational.

And the battle was on.

As Deputy Chris would report back to Brent and Paula, the struggle to get Chris into the back of the cruiser was intense. As they tussled with him, the deputy was finally able to get a cuff on one hand, and then the other. With Chris handcuffed, he eventually relented and allowed them to settle him into the backseat. Deputy Chris sat with Chris AuCoin in the cruiser while the other officers drove back to the station to retrieve the documents that would secure a few more days for Chris to be involuntarily held. It was just the two of them for quite a while, and they got to talking. The young deputy and veteran state trooper had much in common.

"We talked a lot about the stresses of the job," Deputy Chris told Brent and Paula. "I knew Chris was in trouble, but it could happen to any of us."

Chris told the deputy about why he'd joined the Marines. The early innate awareness he'd felt for his life's calling. The common motivators he used to make a positive impact during wartime, and when he taught new troopers how to do the hardest jobs with virtue and honor. The trustworthiness he'd earned as a SWAT commander and NHSP major. How he'd always tried to follow strict standards and decorum both on and off duty.

Deputy Chris was cautious yet sympathetic and well-skilled to de-escalate Chris's heightened state. Once the paperwork was secured and he knew where Chris was going, he personally delivered him to the door. During the drive from the Chili's parking lot to the New Horizons Rehab Center in Fort Pierce, he disclosed to Chris his own concerns about the risks of their chosen career. The toll it took on their families, bodies, and mental health. He told Chris about some specific incidents he'd responded to, and experiences he'd had. The master in the backseat listened, nodded, and… educated.

"He started to critique my tactics." Deputy Chris shared more with Chris's parents. "Actually broke down my moves. To which I told him, 'Well, Chris, who's in the back of the cruiser right now and who's still driving?'"

For whatever reason, Deputy Chris and Chris AuCoin met each other that day and formed a bond of trust—even as one of them was still carving out a legacy in law enforcement and the other had already cemented his.

"But what I remember the most was how he talked about his daughters."

Deputy Chris told Brent and Paula how animated yet sad their son became when he spoke of his deep love for Kelsey, Bethany, and Lindsay. When he delivered Chris to the center's intake area, Deputy Chris wished him well, and thanked him for the mutual respect they'd provided to each other.

The next day, Paula's phone rang. It was Chris's nurse requesting she bring some clothes and specific medications the facility didn't have. Given how irate Chris had been in the voicemails he'd left the day before, she never expected he'd want to see her. But he did.

Carrying a bag with her son's personal items, Paula felt the blood drain from her face as Chris came through the door wearing clothing that wasn't his, his expression distorted by regret, his arms wide and eager to wrap her between them.

"Mom, I'm so scared," he breathed into her shoulder. "I'm so scared."

She shushed and cooed to him like she'd done a million times before after a nightmare or a fight with his brothers back when he was just a boy. She feathered her fingers gently around his neck and felt his rapid pulse next to her own heart. This was her Chris and it took all she had left in her weary psyche to tell him everything would be okay and then walk herself out that door—leaving him all alone on the other side.

When Chris was released from New Horizons several days later, Paula was there to pick him up and drive him back to the townhouse. In the first couple of weeks that followed, Chris traveled to the West Palm VA center for outpatient therapy and to see his personal therapist. He told Paula he wasn't sure if he should stay in Florida or return to New Hampshire to be with his family. One day after a therapy session, Chris announced he'd made his decision.

"Mom, pack your bags. We're going home."

The next morning, they set off for New Hampshire, only stopping when they had to for gas.

CHAPTER TWENTY-ONE
RUNNING MAN

In 2010, Chris completed the 114th running of the Boston Marathon in four hours, seven minutes. Already a notorious fitness nut, Chris had an unorthodox training program for the marathon that was the opposite of how Sean Haggerty was prepping for Boston.

Chris was a fitness freak, and Sean distinctly remembered how he designed crazy training sessions for them at work. At times, he'd have them swimming across the river with backpacks on. It was tough, but Chris required them to meet group standards. When Chris came to Sean, who'd already run Boston many times, he showed up as himself and trained that way.

One morning, Sean was decked out in fancy running gear, apps on his phone, and wore every gadget and piece of specialized clothing runners leaned on to improve time and stamina. But Chris? He showed up on a cold and rainy day wearing sweatpants and a hoodie with two peanut butter and jelly sandwiches tucked into his pocket. And, as Sean remembered, Chris still kicked his ass.

Chris completed the marathon alongside other state troopers as part of a relationship with Massachusetts State Police to raise money for charity. NHSP has competed in the marathon with MASP since 2009, and it remained a priority for Sean through the years.

In 2021, Phil Smith invited Chris to join his wife and family on the route as Phil ran Boston. By then, he was often on the front lines when calls about Chris in distress were made and assistance requested. Phil helped every time he could, as did Kevin Duffy, Chris Vetter, Sean Haggerty, Buddy Hackett, and Kevin Sullivan. They always answered the calls from the AuCoins, because that's what you did for a friend like Chris.

"He, Chris," Phil said one day on the phone, thinking it a nice way to keep Chris engaged in something he loved. "Come to Boston with us. Come watch with the family. I'd love for you to be there."

Chris accepted the invitation, but once he and Phil's family were assembled in place to catch a glimpse of him as he went running by, something happened.

"So, I forgot something in the car," Chris told Phil's wife. He shuffled around, uncomfortable and tense, but stayed with her. Eventually, in the days after the marathon, Phil called him on his odd behavior.

"Were you thinking about leaving?" he asked Chris.

"Yes," he admitted.

Chris told Phil it had taken everything in him that day not to walk away and get lost in Boston.

Chris became a running man, both in the literal and figurative sense. Even when he wasn't sure where he was going.

—★—

Reasoning with Chris, his parents already knew, was often futile, so they were cautious one March evening when he told them he wasn't hungry and refused to eat dinner. Chris had been staying with them then, as he often did, and made several trips upstairs to his room. He'd come back down, sit for a few minutes, get back up, and return to the second floor.

"What's he doing?" Brent asked. "What's going on?"

Paula shrugged, her appetite gone as a worried spin overtook her stomach.

Chris returned to the dining room fully dressed in outdoor survival gear; a stuffed backpack swung over his shoulder.

"I'm leaving," he told them flatly.

"Chris, why? It's getting late. You can't leave, where are you going?"

Brent paused. He held the pleas inside his throat in place, that cue he'd learned the hard way reminding him how rapidly Chris escalated when pushed.

Without another word, Chris collected his belongings and walked out to his truck. It pulled out of the driveway as Brent and Paula looked at each other and shook their heads.

"What do we do now?" she asked.

They later learned Chris had called his brother, Nate, who was building a new house a few miles away. But if Chris left his parents' house intending to stop by the construction site, he either left immediately after or never got there at all.

In the deep dark of night, their phone rang. It was that clanking chime that struck dread in them each time Chris's location was unknown. His voice cracking, Brent answered, and braced for bad news.

"I've heard from Chris," Tracy told him. "He's lost."

"Lost?"

By then, Paula was up and trying to lean over Brent's shoulder to hear for herself. *Lost,* she mouthed in disbelief.

"Somewhere in New York City, he thinks."

"I don't understand…" Brent started.

"He said he was headed for Florida, and had gotten lost," Tracy relayed. "That's all I know."

There were multiple problems with this scenario, and Brent mentally scrolled through them all.

"He doesn't have a license right now," Paula said, though Brent already knew that. Chris often lost his license due to multiple DUI events.

"Is he drunk?"

"Is he hurt?"

"We have to get to him."

They threw on clothes, grabbed their keys, and began the long trek to somewhere in New York City where Chris had become either disoriented or worse. It helped that Chris's daughter, Lindsay, had installed an app on his phone that allowed them to track his location without him knowing.

"Try to figure out where he is," Brent advised Paula as they drove west into New York state. Hours on dark roads went by and Chris remained accessible only on this app. He wasn't answering their calls but clearly had his phone with him and the battery hadn't yet died.

Paula was following Chris's dot on her phone. He had made his way out of New York.

"He's in Pennsylvania," she told Brent. "But he's erratic. First, he's going east on I-80, and then west. Brent, it's like he's getting off the highway and getting right back on, but in the opposite direction."

None of it added up. Chris had driven to Florida too many times to count, plus he'd been a state trooper, and was always behind the wheel of a vehicle. He was not merely proficient as a driver; he was an exceptionally skilled one. An expert with directions.

"What in the world?" she muttered, her eyes transfixed on the tiny orb on her screen. "Chris, what are you doing?"

And when he called them, Chris was unsure himself. Frantic, panicked, lost to time and the seemingly irregular look of the highway spread out in front of him.

"Chris!" Brent picked up. "Where are you?"

"I can't figure this out!" Chris told him, his voice elevated and gravely. He was agitated. Scared, even. "I don't know where I am!"

But Chris hung up before Brent and Paula could tell him to get off the highway and stay put. That they were coming. When the phone rang again it was Tracy, and she had an update.

"He's in New York. He was in an accident and is under arrest," she said. "Other drivers called police and reported the truck weaving across lanes."

It was awful in every way, but Brent and Paula expelled their worry that Chris would hurt himself or someone else when they learned he was off the road and in police custody. At least he was safe. The next step was to keep him that way.

"Please, please, do not put him in jail. Please let us explain." Brent begged the officer at the station where Chris was being detained. "He's suffering from complex PTSD." He described the morbid odyssey they'd been on with Chris, his career in the NHSP, SWAT, and military. "Please, don't put him behind bars."

In the grips of the Covid-19 pandemic, a nearby hospital accepted Chris but kept Brent and Paula out due to strict policies in place. As they waited outside the ER, Paula placed call after call to his VA therapist back in New England, to get Chris discharged from New York, and back into treatment where he'd been previously seen in Bedford, Massachusetts. The calls continued until a breakthrough approval was granted. As Chris exited through the doors of the ER, Paula choked on fresh tears.

"He looks defeated," she whispered to Brent as she clutched her hands around his elbow. "This can't go on."

His parents didn't ask Chris for any explanation or review of the last several hours. They didn't speak much on the ride to the lot where Chris's truck had been impounded. Once they'd cleared it to drive home, he slid into the passenger seat as Brent climbed in behind the wheel. Paula followed behind but a flurry of phone calls changed their plans. His VA team in Bedford was now suggesting they bring Chris to another location in Massachusetts.

"Brockton has a bed available." Paula nodded silently, too tired to engage or request an explanation. As long as Chris could be somewhere, anywhere, where he'd be safe, she would make sure he arrived.

CHAPTER TWENTY-TWO
CYCLICAL AGONY

The unpredictability of Chris became the central theme of his family's world. They were never lulled into a false belief that the good times would last forever, but rather grew to appreciate them moment to moment, and day by day. Chris would wrack up months of sobriety and begin dreaming about his future again. He'd start a business, work it for a while, reunite with his buddies, and then have a bad day, relapse, disappear into the woods, and flame out. It was a ruthless pattern that ensnared everyone who loved Chris.

Chris and Kevin Sullivan reconnected around 2019 when their New Hampshire Marine group got together for reunions. Kevin saw him with Tracy and passed along his contact information. It began a cycle of Chris being drunk for days, entering rehab, and then going off the rails again. Kevin would get a call, go in, and get Chris back on track.

It was unpredictable in that way, and after enduring his own post-deployment struggles, Kevin began a career and purpose as a readjustment counselor for veterans. His life was recalibrated in a way that put helping warriors and first responders deal with trauma and crisis his main goal. He learned how to show them how much stronger they were for their experiences. How resilient in life they'd become, if only they let themselves see it.

Kevin had always considered Chris the solid one. He'd understood hunger, thirst, and being afraid. In that, Chris was the one person he, or anyone, could rely on because he'd never let them down.

And yet, Chris packed all his pain so deep inside himself, Kevin never expected he would be the one to crack. And that his own family would be in his crosshairs. One incident the prior year was another shocking example of how bad things had become.

—★—

Just before 6:30 on a beautiful late September evening in 2018, Paula called 9-1-1 and asked to speak to an officer. The police report indicated she wouldn't elaborate, but Paula had to act fast. Tracy had called earlier with a warning.

"Just a heads up," Tracy told them. "Chris is very drunk and having a bad day here at home. He just took off in his truck and told me he was coming out to your house. He says he's going to burn it down."

County dispatch knew Chris, the AuCoins, and the history of depression, PTSD, substance abuse, violence, and arrests, so when Paula called back again with an update, they prepared to respond with an abundance of caution.

"Let's move the cars," Brent told Paula, panicked and fearful, as they often were by then. It wasn't fear for themselves; it was that loathsome uncertainty of how far Chris would go, and what it would take to make him stop.

"We can make sure one of the cars faces either side of the road in case Chris blocks us in and we have to get out fast."

They scurried around the yard and arranged one vehicle to face toward one exit, and the other facing the road on the driveway's second exit to the street. The house sat between two roads, which was convenient in case Chris's truck blocked one of their vehicles, they'd have an additional option to escape. Racing through Paula's mind was another recent incident at home with Chris, who spent weeks or sometimes months with them when Tracy wasn't comfortable having him home with her and their girls.

With Brent still working, she was often alone with Chris until her husband got home at night. Some days, Chris was docile and calm, reading the Bible at the table as they sat down together and had coffee. He'd been working construction and getting out in the fresh air. But other days, he was restless, dour, and threatening. He'd become desensitized to typical red flags, like the safety risk of burning a fire in their small fireplace that had roared too big and bright. Paula knew the huge inferno Chris had built was far too large for the tiny box to handle, yet she was scared to say that to him. She'd sat and watched that fire until it had burned itself out, thankful it hadn't slipped out of its confined space and up the walls. Now, drunken Chris was envisioning exactly what she'd feared: a fire so powerful it would destroy their home. It was wholly mortifying to imagine.

"Brent, go, go!" she ordered him out with one set of keys as she took another. "I'll go to the back exit."

She'd described Chris's truck to the police and the likely back road route he'd take to their house. Then, she and Brent went outside and waited. They waited for the police.

And they waited for Chris.

The police report from that day confirms police arrived at the AuCoin house and discovered two cars strategically placed in different directions off the driveway. It also describes an update to the BOLO, the *Be on the Lookout* warning they'd released for Chris's truck to include Paula's concern that he could be armed and may go somewhere to harm himself. As the officers at the house stayed with Brent and Paula, the other unit was relaying new information through radio traffic.

"Two officers are responding to an accident. Vehicle matches BOLO description of Chris's truck."

Brent's heart slammed against his ribs while Paula pressed for more details. "Is he hurt?" she begged the officer. "Is Chris okay?"

"There's a subject outside the vehicle walking around," the officer told her. The AuCoins then had a warning for them all.

"You tell those officers to be careful." They spoke in unison, one over the other to relay critical advice. "Chris is very strong. Please tell them to be careful around him."

They knew Chris best, and in the drunken state of mind he was in that day, they were right. The officers needed to be careful.

—★—

According to the police report, Chris's behavior rapidly deteriorated once he was taken into police custody on a DUI arrest. The unit assigned to the accident scene found massive tire disruption to the road's shoulder and sheared bark from the trunk of a tree, with Chris's truck damaged and dented. Radio traffic indicated the unit transporting Chris was expediting to the police department with lights and siren both activated, which meant Chris was getting out of control.

The report describes Chris, at first, mumbling and grunting, slumped over with no shoes on. He was placed in a chair in the booking room when he slammed his hands down on the desk, tried to stand up and push himself away from it. Officers raced over to subdue and restrain Chris, yet he was like a bull—railing against their grip, he thrashed and thwarted their efforts to secure a restraining belt and ankle chains. Finally, with Chris's head braced on one officer's thigh to prevent him from banging it on the ground, they picked him up and sat him back in his chair.

"Take these off me!" Chris yelled and demanded the cuffs come off. "Take them off right now!"

The struggle revealed a new squalor. Chris's pants showed a wet spot of urine, and a small stream of blood had trickled out from his head. The officers used toilet paper to clean that up and wipe away the superficial scratch. As the adrenaline stopped pumping, the alcohol's effect had Chris losing consciousness in the chair. The officers moved Chris to a cell, placed him on a bench, and reported several emotional cycles that followed.

In what was described as his angry phase, Chris stood up and attempted to push away from officers who were nearby. He'd spit and swear, hurl insults and derogatory slurs, challenge them to a fight, and attempt to order them around. Each time Chris tried to physically push on the officers or try to get back up, they'd hold him down until he was calm.

The depressive phase followed. Chris was contrite, remorseful, and as tears streamed down his face he'd talk about the problems in his life. At one point during this phase, he put his head down, closed his eyes, and repeatedly stated, "Make it end."

During Chris's submissive phase, he would agree to whatever the officers asked him to do. But that was temporary, and over the course of his stay in that cell, he'd cycle back through each phase multiple times.

One time, when Chris was angry, an ambulance crew was called to check on him, though he was too combative and refused to cooperate. Ultimately, he was ruled a refusal for medical treatment.

Less than a month later, Chris was at a retreat in Brattleboro, Vermont when he passed out on a bench in the hallway, unable to be woken. Once emergency medical services were on scene, Chris became alert, conscious, and enraged.

"Who the fuck are you?" he bellowed. Bristling to their touch and defiant, Chris finally agreed to a hospital transport and passed out for the entire ride.

As quickly as one horrible event ended, another would begin. One hospital ER turned into two, sometimes three in multiple states at all hours. Friends came by, stayed, but always had to leave to return to their own lives. Chris, like clockwork, ticked back to unbridled pain. Relapsed.

And the cycle continued.

Once, Brent and Paula coaxed Chris into the car after another relapse and drunken skid. They were maxing out locations and services and determined getting him back to Vermont—where Chris's history was well known—was their best option. Paula drove, Chris was in the passenger seat, with Brent in the back. The man he'd once called the strongest he'd ever known, was now the recipient of Chris's simmering resentment.

"You know, Dad. You never took care of our family business. You are so weak, Dad." Chris's eyes were slits; his mouth contorted around sour and detestable proclamations. Brent sat there and took his son's venom, knowing all the while he had to. Whatever it took to get Chris back into treatment. He remained mostly silent as the goading went on, only asking one simple question of his son.

"Chris, why are you doing this?"

But no answer would ever fit, not that Chris could articulate the blackness that had invaded his thoughts. He pushed his dad. Pushed and gnashed at him. Insults and vitriol.

"Hit me, Dad. Go ahead, hit me."

Chris wanted the first physical engagement to come from Brent, so he could then unload all the pain out of himself, and onto another. Because it was so sharp and thorny, Chris could not hold it all by himself.

"Mom, pull over!" he ordered. "Pull over so I can fight Dad!"

Chris tore the buckle of his seat belt off and swept his chest toward Brent in the back seat as his arm went over the headrest. As his hand connected with Brent's face, the awareness of what had just happened coursed through the car. Chris had struck his father. He'd hit Brent! Everything around them silenced, even as Paula knew she was yelling at Chris to stop, trying to see if Brent was okay, to keep the car on the road, and manage the rapid fire of her own heartbeat.

Chris had become unrecognizable to his parents. A beast, according to one of his daughters. A force they no longer recognized. Once Brent and Paula had dropped Chris back off at the VA in Vermont, they drove home in that shared absence of present state, an emotional hypoesthesia that paralyzed every thought minus one: *How much more can we take?*

Paula's voice sounded like glass breaking.

"How is this going to end?" she asked, though fully aware it was unanswerable. "All these places, Brent. All these places we've found to take him, they're not helping. We keep trying to find places but then there's another problem and then we're back in solution mode. When will we ever have peace?"

Brent stared out at the blurry trees as they passed by. He didn't attempt a response, yet knew he and Paula would never, could never stop trying. He maintained that attitude for a decade, as Chris fell back into a relapse, got arrested, called in backup in the form of friends, specialists, SWAT and Marine colleagues. Every single one of them would drop what they were doing and rush in. They'd find Chris in a hotel room, or being held in a jail waiting to be transported somewhere else. They never stopped answering the bell—even as it rang and rang, at all hours, nearby and far away.

"Chris, you're not alone in this."

"Hey, buddy, setbacks are part of recovery. You'll get there."

"We love you, Chris, what do you need right now?"

Everyone who loved Chris empowered him to articulate his needs.

They provided comfort and took care. They showed up, stayed, checked in, and laced up their boots to march through underbrush, snow, puddles, and mud when Chris disappeared for days into the woods. Experts in addiction, PTSD, trauma, military and law enforcement flashbacks, talk therapy, SSRI drugs, and AA gatherings watched Chris have moments of lucidity—when the former man appeared to be just behind the curtain, using all his strength to pull it back so his true self could be seen again. But then, his grip would weaken, his stamina fell, his resolve slipped away. Time and again, his parents watched their son flail and fumble, like a drowning man gasping for a last gulp of air just before a rogue wave, towering off in the distance, got closer.

And closer.

Kevin Sullivan had a special knack for getting Chris back on track, but he was tougher on him that most others dared to be. He refused to enable Chris, even as he begged for another day to taper off.

"Negative," Kevin would tell him. He knew helping Chris meant never relenting on his position. There was no tapering off, there was only right now, and Kevin never backed down.

Chris lived with Kevin a couple of times and the two former Marines once again grew very close. Buddy Hackett called it a special relationship between the two, and that Kevin wanted to help Chris in his own way. He would get the call to help Chris, and sometimes he alone, or with Buddy and others, would get him out.

Buddy and his fellow Marines considered that a profound pact they'd made with each other the moment they stepped foot on foreign soil. He'd battled his own addictions, illnesses, and hopelessness, so whenever Chris slipped, Buddy felt his agony, too. That hurried race back to the bottom of a bottle. The wasted dream that had been glued back together—only so it could shatter a thousand more times. The visage of hateful regret that stared back at him from a streaky mirror.

He told Chris he would sit with him forever.

That everything was going to be okay.

"We're brothers and that's what brothers do," he'd say.

Kevin's tact was similar, deliberate, based in his own research, and fully hands-on.

CHAPTER TWENTY-THREE
MUTUAL AID

Kevin called Chris lucid for most of the time he stayed with him. While Chris had it in his head, and Kevin supported it, that he was coming to visit. To help Kevin in some way. They tried to take care of each other.

When Chris stayed with Kevin, he'd land in the apartment down in the basement. He had a TV down there and would take time to stabilize, stay for a couple of days, and have dinner with Kevin's kids.

But many times, Chris also came to drink.

"Hey, bud, you've had a lot already today," Kevin lied. Chris was drinking and on medication. Kevin was wary of the mixing and Chris's tendency to overdo it. "You know if you start acting weird again, I'm taking you to the doctor."

"Yeah, yeah, Sully. I'm good, man. I'm good."

For the most part, Chris was quiet when he was with Kevin, tired and unwilling to wrestle with the rules of the house. But not always. There was one incident that started bad and got worse. Kevin got a call from Tracy.

"Sully, Chris is gone. He's taken off somewhere."

Kevin located Chris, very drunk and stumbling through shallow woods. He pulled him out and loaded him into his truck to get him back to Kevin's house.

"Hey, man, let's get some food. I'm hungry."

"Okay, Chris—" Kevin was agreeable to that, but before he could supply Chris with a quick burger and fries from a drive through, he bolted out of the passenger door and took off running down the road.

"Chris!"

Kevin found him again about a block away, pulled up to the bar of some joint, with a drink in his hand.

"Hey, Sully! Come here, sit down, have a drink with me!"

While it was impressive how rapidly Chris had gotten himself out of Kevin's truck and onto that barstool, Kevin was in no mood to drink with him and sensed the atmosphere turning tense. Chris was loud and other patrons were starting to watch him. Kevin had to get Chris back to his place before things went south.

"Pal, we gotta go," he started.

"No! Sully, have a drink."

"Chris, we need to get going. I'll have a soda and you finish your drink, then we're leaving."

But Chris refused. And, predictably, became irritated and argumentative with other people at the bar. But first, with Kevin.

"I'll fight you, man. I'll fight you right now. I'm not leaving!"

Kevin used his counselor's training and his decades long friendship with Chris to turn his anger into a radical explanation.

"If you take a swing at me, Chris, it won't end well and you know it. You could really hurt me. Do you want to hurt me, Chris?" Kevin stood his ground. While he'd stand shoulder to shoulder with Chris every time he needed him, Kevin would never allow himself to be railroaded. Chris decided against a scuffle with his dear friend, but that urge to squabble and rabble-rouse was still potent. He spoke to a manager, and then a woman who said something to her boyfriend. And from there, it all went to hell.

"Back off, man," the boyfriend told Chris. "Don't mess with us. I'm a veteran."

Kevin closed his eyes and let out a huge sigh. That was about the worst thing the guy could have said to make Chris's fuse burn lower.

"Oh, really?" Chris pushed back, sarcasm laced through his tone. "You're a veteran, are you?"

Kevin felt the air thicken around him. His muscles locked in place, prepared to either block Chris's access to the boyfriend, or take the punch himself.

"Back off," Kevin warned the nameless man. "Back off, or you'll have to fight both of us."

The manager had seen enough and asked Kevin and Chris to leave.

Kevin bear hugged Chris and dragged him outside. "Chris, get in the truck!"

"No!"

As Chris took off again, Kevin realized he was outmatched. He needed help to ensure the night didn't degrade further.

He'd maintained relationships with local police he'd met through work, and frankly, through Chris's many scuffles, arrests, and protective holds. He called his friends at the Manchester police department and asked for assistance. With no choice left, and an unwillingness to leave Chris out there for the night, Kevin accepted he could not manage him on his own.

The officers helped to find Chris and held him until the next morning. When they showed up at Kevin's workplace, the Veteran's Center in the next town over, to hand Chris over to him, Kevin maintained that shoulder-to-shoulder position he'd assumed so many times before. He set Chris up in his office where he fell into a deep sleep. He was not about to allow the police to come wake him up and haul him away. Kevin couldn't let Chris stay very long, but he asked the officers not to drag him back out, but rather to do it his way.

"I'll wake him up and walk him peacefully out to your car. He's half-asleep right now, and if you insist on going in to get him, you're going to have to fight us both."

The officers agreed to allow Kevin to accompany Chris out, and once he was safely secured in their vehicle, they took him to the hospital where he stayed overnight. Kevin was right there in the courtroom when Chris appeared the following day. He told the judge he didn't want to fight Kevin, that he was sorry. That he was struggling. The usual post-incident remorse had set in.

When they saw each other outside, they talked privately and apologized to each other through tears.

"We'll figure it out," Kevin said. "Like we always do."

"Okay, Kev. Okay."

Brothers forever.

When Brent and Paula called Kevin again, to help them remove Chris from a hotel room in Nashua where he'd been holed up for days, he entered the room first, with Brent. To both get Chris squared away before his family saw him, and to clean up the room.

Kevin did that for his friend, but also for his family. Not only had Chris's parents arrived at the hotel, but they'd also been accompanied by Tracy, and their daughters. His entire family had shown up for Chris. Time and time again.

Most families would have asked Kevin to go and get Chris himself, but not the AuCoins. The whole family was going to try and help him, even when they didn't get along. They remained totally aligned when it came to him. In Kevin's experience he didn't see that a lot. The commitment was exceptional.

Kevin had worked with combat veterans in crisis, some for months or years, and he'd been trained to look for certain things. One was family support, which tended to wane the longer a loved one remained volatile, addicted to alcohol or drugs, or wholly disruptive and combative. It wasn't to be selfish or to give up hope that things could get better, but rather to survive. While Chris never spoke to Kevin about the strain his PTSD and drinking had put on his family, or why he'd lash out the hardest at the ones he loved the most, Kevin's education had taught him how common it was. Because when someone loves you the way a family member does, the door never fully shuts.

He came up with a theory when family members took abuse from someone they loved. He told it like this: "A baby will bite the safest person, right? Because that person won't bite back. A mom won't bite her baby back; she'll try to figure out what's wrong. Biting, in this case, is the inability to communicate what's wrong. I don't believe Chris knew how to tell the people he loved the most what he was feeling."

Tracy had those bite marks everywhere. When Chris was at his worst, he was manipulative, judgmental, accusatory. He'd blame her for the distrust his daughters felt toward him, twisting it to make her believe it was her fault, and never his.

"You're brainwashing them!" he'd claim.

She'd helped Chris detox from pain and anxiety medications, yet alcohol dependency lingered like a phantom buzz in a body part long separated from its original place. Chris had sustained himself on beer, just a few a day in the early years, to maintain operational function during his time on SWAT and when he was perpetually on call. On vacations, he'd go hard.

She suspected Chris was likely already an alcoholic when she first met him. When they'd take a vacation or go somewhere with the goal of relaxing and unwinding from the rigors of work, Chris would become too intoxicated to even be around. She was frustrated and worried.

The more work responsibility Chris was handed; he got tighter with his drinking but could not go a day without it. Tracy and his parents would attempt to talk him out of that, telling him how powerful he was, that he could do anything.

"So why can't you go a day without beer?" Tracy asked.

But Chris couldn't.

Tracy began to set protective boundaries for herself and the girls, even though Chris called her selfish. It became harder to separate what she heard from him when he was drunk versus what he really believed. Scars formed around her heart, from sleepless nights when Chris was somewhere, drunk, threatening he'd harm himself, not answering his phone. When he did come home, he'd go to bed for days on end. The entire family worried, but Tracy began to ask, *what about us?*

Incident after incident, and year after year. When Chris barricaded himself in his parents' garage, and Paula called 9-1-1. When he was tased and dropped to his knees on the hardened winter ground, begging them to make it stop.

"Mom, Dad, help me!"

Visions and hallucinations. When Chris had locked all the windows and doors at the Old Orchard Beach house and refused to answer his phone. As Brent found him the next morning, Chris was convinced he was holding off Iraqis on the beach. He went room by room to scour for the enemy. When he'd call Tracy, three times, fifteen times, expressing his intent to harm himself, she remained steadfast and applied the logic he'd always, at least to that point, listened to.

"The girls need you!" Tracy told him. "You can't do this, Chris."

And yet there were still distinct times when Chris was patently Chris: funny, gracious, smart, and at one time, a stabilizing force for the neighbor across the street who'd just lost her husband to suicide. What he'd said to her, in retrospect, was eerily prophetic.

"Chris went to sit with her," Tracy remembered. "He told her how her husband wasn't thinking of her when he was that despondent. Chris imparted to her, his own thoughts."

CHAPTER TWENTY-FOUR
RIPPER UNDER CONSTRUCTION

Following the New York highway incident, the VA in Brockton, Massachusetts kept Chris for several weeks. Brent and Paula were eventually allowed to take Chris off premises and out to lunch.

"Feels sort of strange to be out," he told them as they sat down in a booth. Chris had been quiet on the drive over to a restaurant they'd selected randomly. Introspective and reflective of the series of events that had landed him there. His chin supported on his palm, Chris seemed reposeful yet clear-minded. They waited for him to make conversation, not sure in which direction he'd move.

"They're strict here," he said finally. "I have a routine."

Brent and Paula nodded. "That's probably the best thing for you right now, Chris."

They all felt well-versed in what created the sturdiest cohesion in Chris. Recovery had a certain rhythm to it, and when Chris was able to monitor himself within those guardrails, he did quite well.

"Stability is key, Chris," Paula continued. "Putting days together, and then weeks, months. That's how you'll get stronger. How you'll get back to the girls."

Chris nodded into his hand, his mouth breaking into something close to a tight smile. "I know, Mom."

Chris left the VA in Brockton on April 14th, 2021, and remained sober for some time. For the first time in many years, Brent and Paula had the audacity to believe a brighter future was in sight. That door they refused to shut, was thrust wide open for hope to burst back in.

—★—

The routine was delivering results, or more of a safety net that swung just beneath the trademark unpredictability associated with addiction, PTSD, stress, and an overburdened mental load. Even something as simple as a good night's sleep contributed to the delicate evenness of Chris's stability, though this time, he was helping himself in ways he had failed to before. That started with a vision for what his life could look like, and a harkening back to who he'd always been at his core: A helper who desired to serve others, who loved the natural world around him, his family, and being physically adept. Chris began to pave his road back with a self-designed program bulked up by daily AA meetings and therapy sessions, power lifting in the gym, biking for miles, swimming, fly fishing, hiking the steep faces of New Hampshire's mountains, and using his durable carpenter's hands to build, dubbing the business, TF Ripper Construction. But there was more. Chris began to recognize an intellectual stirring in himself, one that could further support his family, which was always his goal. Work that could combine all his pain, humiliation, failures, and therapy and then use that to ward off catastrophe and ruin in someone else.

"I want to be a counselor," he told Tracy and his parents. "I want to get my master's, and I want to help other veterans and first responders."

They all thought Chris would make a fantastic counselor. Chris was a leader in rehab, and his AA meetings. A highlight for people to look up to. If he could've been a professional patient, he would have excelled. Tracy knew whenever Chris had a job to do, it became his everything. Becoming a counselor, she believed, would have been exactly like that.

But intuitively, she also knew the more Chris bit off, the more pressure he'd feel, and the risk of a relapse always loomed. He was also flipping houses under his business, Ripper Construction, and the busier he got, the more pieces there were for Tracy to put back together as he fell apart.

Chris was like a speeding train, she thought. Either everyone got on board with whatever he wanted, or they had to get out of the way.

She was handling the kids, their rental properties, and—when Chris was detoxing during the process of preparing a flip in Jaffrey—Tracy had to work from Wilton while it was waiting to close, until Chris was well enough to attend. She also decided against allowing any other children at their house. There was always some compensation to make for Chris.

There was one time when she had to explain to a mom whose daughter was over at their house. Chris was in a bad way, it got loud and tense, and she, in good conscience, no longer allowed their daughters to have other kids over. It was difficult not just for her; their girls' world got smaller as a result.

As 2022 arrived, that fragile safety net beneath them began to fray even more.

And then split wide open.

CHAPTER TWENTY-FIVE
HEART HOLES

A behavioral therapist in the Autism program, Tracy worked the summer school session that year. Chris had moved back into their Wilton home after highly upsetting news he'd received during a recent visit to the doctor. He needed open heart surgery. Another physical and mental setback on an already rickety balance beam of sobriety. Any time Chris had achieved even a short absence from alcohol, his family worried about stressors or triggers that could jeopardize it, and this surgery felt huge.

But as one friend told Tracy: where there's life, there is hope. And she maintained that position even as Chris faced yet another medical setback.

It surprised her when their youngest daughter, Lindsay, who adored her father, chose not to visit much while he was in the hospital for a week after surgery to repair a hole in his heart. Tracy figured she'd accompany Lindsay during visits but then stayed away when her daughter made that decision for herself. Chris had been suicidal for most of Lindsay's childhood, and while he was being closely monitored in the hospital, Tracy reasoned that gave her daughter a sense of peace. She knew where her dad was and that he was safe.

Brent and Paula visited daily. It was a massive surgery, and Chris was in tremendous pain. Even still, he called Tracy days before he was scheduled to be released and told her he wanted to come home early. It was a Sunday, and Tracy set about cleaning the house for his arrival. Chris preferred the house clean and she wanted him to be as comfortable as possible when he returned. She wanted to be prepared for whatever he would need as he recovered.

When Chris was cleared to leave the hospital, he came home but felt a measure of resentment that she hadn't visited. Tracy declined to engage, even when Chris pushed and threatened her that he'd take the girls if they split. She called that drunk talk and set a hard boundary with Chris—even as it took a toll on her.

Tracy had done all she could to keep the girls away from the worst moment, arguments, and incidents, but it was coming up on a decade and much of it, she realized, had tainted their childhood. She'd rushed them out of their home many times, to take refuge in a hotel, or her parents' home, all while keeping them on schedule, in school, and safe. But theirs was a family in crisis, and it wore them down. As Chris was constantly supported, delivered to rehab, picked up from protective custody, consoled, and unconditionally loved, Tracy often felt left behind, scared, and entirely alone to raise her girls. With Chris home recovering, she felt suffocated by how energetically low he was, and how tight that made her. While it was civil, there was no affection, and that evolved into a crushing realization that Chris likely didn't want to be near her at all. She maintained her job, appreciated all the help from Brent and Paula, and did all she could—to the extent possible—to get Chris stronger as he healed. She accompanied him on every appointment, used her nursing skills to wean him off pain medications, and watched for new signs of drinking. Her own heart, managing holes of a different sort. She grieved the husband of long ago. She wished for the father and provider he'd been to return. She accepted that being there for Chris was taking years off her own life. If she failed to protect herself, she feared she'd go down, too.

As summer gave way to fall, and Chris got his strength back, he began to slip. All those months of sobriety would be washed away by a relapse. But then, another brief sobriety when Chris renewed his focus and energy on his new goal of becoming a counselor.

But then, Chris would slip again.

CHAPTER TWENTY-SIX
A BRITTLE FALL

Chris's middle daughter, Bethany, felt a shift in her father when he was drinking again. Just looking at him, she'd know. It was a weirdness, she sensed, but chastised herself for overreacting. Was Chris over the edge yet? Whenever Chris drank for the first time after being sober, Bethany could tell.

When someone you loved was an alcoholic, time tracked differently. It was a fair practice to separate it into categories: When Dad was good. When Dad was drinking. Bethany called the multiple stretches of Chris's sobriety and relapse *different* each time. If he was sober, she wondered if he also thought of himself differently, and whether he longed for the alternative state of being drunk. She'd seen him drink so much she often thought it altered his brain chemistry.

And she was onto something there, at least scientifically speaking.

Studies have shown the entire body absorbed alcohol, but the brain took the biggest hit. If even light drinking interfered with the communication pathways our brains used to transfer information and perception, Bethany imagined how badly warped her father's had become.

For many years, that concept of time involved her mother, too. Bethany often played the role of peacemaker in her family, more to protect

Tracy and keep her safe as Chris became agitated and angry. That *time* Bethany sat with Chris and talked him down from the nasty accusations he hurled at her mom. That other *time* when she'd had to mentally compartmentalize the fear over where her dad had disappeared to, because worrying about him was debilitating. That *time* when she was young, just a kid, and yet intrinsically knew her father was losing himself to his disease. Losing who he was and letting go of the fierce protector and provider he'd once been for Tracy. For Bethany and her two sisters.

While Bethany was hopeful a counseling career would click for her father, it was that personal refinement of time that led her to a more pensive, contemplative position. Time, for Bethany, had shown a blatant pattern she and everyone who loved Chris couldn't ignore.

During Thanksgiving of 2022, Chris drank the entire week. Chad hosted that year, and on November 24th, Brent and Paula sat with their family and watched Chris gulp down alcohol, even as an important event in his master's program drew closer. An event that would require sobriety and clear-headedness.

On November 27th, 2022, Chris arrived at his hotel in Nashua for an in-house practicum with his psychology cohort. The pressure of being away from home—where temptations and distractions were abundant, had caused more friction between Chris and Tracy.

She talked to him several times that week to ensure he felt ready, but in the end, Tracy believed Chris put himself in that position. He argued how he was required to be there, but never came up with Plan B. What he would do if he felt pressured or stressed. And Tracy, who lived by the same quadrant of time that her daughters did--when Chris was sober versus when Chris was drunk--reasoned something else had come to his mind.

Chris really wanted to go to the practicum, and she couldn't convince herself it wasn't so that he could freely drink there.

Brent and Paula also marked time in their own way. Time between incidents, arrests, rehab, emergencies, surgeries, recoveries, breakdowns, escapes, shame, hope, and futility. As that practicum week in Nashua rolled from Monday, into Tuesday, and so on, they felt more confident that Chris was holding his own. The master's psychology program he was enrolled in held the retreat for students to role-play, share ideas, and discuss various events in their lives. They all knew Chris was a rock star in any therapy type setting, and helping others maneuver through their feelings, pain, fear, and frustrations was what he'd always done best.

Then came December.

—★—

On December 1st, the cohort held a karaoke night in the hotel bar. Attendance was required.

Chris drank.

Tracy would call the time, when Chris was in between one or two beers, a sweet spot. When he'd become the old Chris. *There you are,* she'd tell him, and with tears in her eyes, accept the love, affection, and gentleness he'd shown her so long ago. But Chris never could stay in that in-between for very long, and he didn't that night in Nashua.

Somewhere between one or two drinks, and many more that followed, Chris and the instructor at the retreat got into an altercation. Chris, still drunk the next morning, refused to come down from his room to join the rest of the class. When staff tried to intervene, it escalated again and the police were called to remove Chris and bring him to a nearby hospital.

On December 3rd, Chris was released from the hospital and Tracy drove him home. Brent and Paula stayed away that weekend to give Chris and Tracy time alone—for him to sleep and recover from the incident and examine next steps. The following Monday, December 5th, they traveled to Chris's house in Wilton and took him out to lunch. He sat on one side of a booth at the Wilton pizza place, brooding and quiet, staring at the food he didn't eat.

"Chris, you have to figure out what happens next," Paula said quietly. In that mother's way, she sensed in her son something larger than regret over his behavior at the practicum. It felt somehow directed at her. But why? He wouldn't answer. Wouldn't look at her.

"Chris." Brent prompted. "Your mother is talking to you."

Some mothers never lost that magical ability to see through the gauzy and grizzled curtain that grew around their adult children when life tainted them with callouses and hardship. That day, as she sat in the swooped hard plastic of a pizza shop's booth, with her grown son across from her, Paula's heart beat out memories. She lifted the curtain on Chris and saw through it, beyond it, back to the moment he was laid in her arms, red-faced and squirming against the abrupt separation from her body. As adult Chris, so broken and bleary, glared at her from across the booth, Paula saw him on Fern's back, and then graduating from high school, defiantly determined to follow his dreams. Chris, in uniform. Leading NHSP SWAT. A father himself. A law enforcement hero and mentor. So much more—better and worse—than her sixteen-year-old self could have imagined he'd be. If adult Chris wasn't suddenly raising his voice at her, so, so angry, Paula might have smiled. So lost to the tenderness of her love for Chris, she didn't hear him speaking to her.

"…that it was you, Mom. It was you."

Paula's mind snapped itself back into that booth. "Huh? What did I do, Chris? I don't know what you mean." What was Chris saying?

Chris's eyes narrowed. "That's what they told me, Mom. That you were the one who requested the involuntary hold at the hospital. You wanted to keep me there. It was you!"

Paula's hands went up. No, no, no, that wasn't true. "No, Chris. I… I did nothing of the sort, I—"

"Yes, you did!"

Brent's instinct was to insert himself between his wife and son, and he tried to convince Chris what he'd been told was not true, that Paula hadn't requested the hold, at least not that time, and whoever had told him that was wrong. But Chris was raw, coming down from the shame of relapse and the burden of guilt that closed the loop on the endless circle of the past ten years. If he couldn't yet blame himself for the Nashua incident, he had to put that liability somewhere, load it onto someone else. Paula felt it hit her with all the power of a physical blow breaking through skin and bone. Her chest recoiled and her lungs tightened.

"Chris. No." The words were flat, coming out of her sounding as tired and miserable as she felt. "No."

They drove back to Chris's house in silence. Paula never pushed Chris when he was this mad, though she tried, yet again, to convince him there was hope, that he was loved beyond measure, and that his life still had the potential for happiness, fulfillment, and peace. Like they'd done many times before, they invoked the inescapable pain and far-reaching repercussions of whatever alternative plan for a self-imposed finality he was hatching.

"Chris, you have no idea what this would do to your family," Paula said in a hushed whisper from the front seat. "Your father—" she hesitated on the imagined destruction of her husband. "Your father couldn't bear it."

I could not bear it.

They turned off the street and pulled into the long driveway that led to Chris's house. It was quiet. The girls were inside. Chris pulled the handle of the door but held himself inside his parents' car. A few seconds passed, as though both sides were unsure of how to part ways. Brent put the car in park and stepped out, crossing in front of the hood to reach Chris as he left his seat. Paula watched them hug but stayed where she was. That curtain around Chris was back and it draped over him like a leaden shawl of torment. As dark and weighty as any plague humankind could face.

"I love you," she spoke through the window. *I will always love you, Chris.*

She shuddered though the heat that was on. She felt ice cold in her warm car. It was the most brittle fall she could remember, though the metaphorical sensation that had spread through her family had nothing to do with seasonality—only heartache.

As Brent reversed the car and headed back down the driveway, Paula watched Chris climb the front steps, close the door, and disappear inside. Despite so much of the last decade with Chris being chronicled by time, both good and bad, Paula didn't think to mark that moment in her mind. Perhaps because it felt too large, too inconceivable to do so.

Because if she had, it would have gone down as the last time she ever saw him.

CHAPTER TWENTY-SEVEN
PAVING OVER THE HEAVES

On Tuesday, December 6th, 2022, Brent went back to Chris's house under the guise of fixing the driveway. Paula stayed home. She was still upset about Chris's accusations that she'd tried to orchestrate his forced hospital stay, but even more so about his state of mind and public relapse. The fallout was proving to be barbed and taut. Chris was at risk of being permanently bounced from the master's program.

"So, Chris, see here, these heaves need to be dug out, right? We'll need some new gravel around the frost line." Brent tried to pull Chris from his own thoughts, but he was disinterested in the driveway repair and did not participate in the conversation with the paver who'd come by to check out the job.

"Yeah, Dad. Sure. Got it."

Brent didn't care one bit about the driveway either but needed a reason to come by. He needed to lay eyes on his son. To touch his arm. To gauge his level of despair and depression. How deeply had Chris sunk? Like the driveway, the holes and heaves in his family felt like craters no tar could fill.

"He had become fixated with trying to fix the mess he'd created at the Nashua practicum. He'd launched a flurry of emails to the college, and it wasn't looking good." Brent went through the motions of driveway prep work, walked around with the paver and pointed out areas of note, even as Chris disassociated from them both. Once the paver was gone, Brent tried another avenue.

"Let's go inside, Chris. Let's talk a bit."

Chris fell into a chair around the dining room table and put his hands over his face. "I've been working on this letter, Dad."

"Okay, what sort of letter?"

Chris sighed. "An apology. An explanation. I'm going to email it over as soon as I finish working on it."

But the college was communicating with Chris, too.

—★—

Lindsay AuCoin, the youngest of Chris and Tracy's three girls, was about to turn nineteen-years-old in December of 2022. She had been so little when Chris went through thyroid cancer, an elementary school kid, who was protected and kept away from the worst moments by her mom and sisters. While she was too young to know Chris was an alcoholic before his bout with thyroid cancer, there were many problems stirring within her family beyond his health. She had troubling memories, but others that she referred to as untarnished, especially if she went looking for them in her mind. In those early years of her life, Chris was goofy, loving, fun, and happy. At least to her.

As the youngest daughter, Lindsay had more of an unblemished relationship with Chris, whom she called, *the couch monster*, when they'd huddle up together to watch TV or hang out. One time Chris built her a candy corn bike she considered priceless. There was nothing he couldn't do, and Lindsay awoke early every Saturday morning to carry out a dad-and-Lindsay-only tradition: Hit Dunks together, just the two of them. She'd munch on doughnuts, Chris would have coffee, and they'd chat about whatever came to mind. School. Friends. Her sisters and mom. Back then, Lindsay was still wrapped in that blissful childhood innocence her sisters had outgrown. But she would realize, soon enough, that her dad was not like other dads, and her family had been shielding her from a horrible truth. For her, it never was good or stable during Chris's cancer battle, or thereafter.

Lindsay was recognizing patterns with her dad, ones that he didn't think she saw. Even as he was coming home from the hospital, he'd ask to stop at a gas station and return with a brown paper bag. He didn't think she was aware of that, that he was always buying and hiding his alcohol. But Lindsay knew.

She also noticed that Chris would be gone for stretches of time. When he came back, it seemed confusing to her. They'd visit him in sterile hospital rooms, in different states, and she knew he was often at her grandparents' house in Jaffrey. But to a child, instability and dysfunction from an alcoholic and mentally unwell parent rooted deep, and Lindsay—looking back—can recognize when it started to change her.

As a small child, she had moments of panic. She'd race to his room to check on him. To see him and touch his arm, to watch his chest rise with breaths. Lindsay fell into a cycle of being anxious all the time.

She called the summer of 2022 awful.

Chris was bedridden for most of it, which meant he couldn't work out. No gym. No weights. Just sitting in the house, day after day.

While Lindsay doesn't recall Chris ever talking to her about his feelings prior to that summer, once he started to unload them onto her and her sisters, it was difficult to hear how broad and polluted they sounded. By the time of his heart surgery, the AuCoin family had become desensitized to hospitalizations, trouble, and Chris being sick. In that, Lindsay figured her dad felt as though everyone was letting him down, not visiting him as much as they could, not supporting him. Manufactured feelings that grew and pent up inside him.

That pernicious energy spun through the house when Chris came home from the hospital, upset, and hurt. Tracy and the girls, also upset and perpetually hurt, helped as much as they could. When Lindsay and Bethany went to Montreal together for a week, they returned to find out

Chris had relapsed. Dried out. Then relapsed a month later. That time, he was angry with them for not being there for him.

"He'd say we don't appreciate him," Lindsay remembered. "But I always had the biggest soft spot for my dad out of all of us. I was often the only one who could get through to him."

Lindsay was also the daughter who used her technological savvy to keep a constant watch over where Chris was. She downloaded an app onto his phone when he was in the hospital. He never found out it was there.

Bethany called that tracking app her sister downloaded a *game changer* for her family. While Chris never figured it out, Lindsay made sure to turn off notifications. She tracked him constantly. Bethany believed that app is why Chris lived so long.

A couple of days before Chris set off into the woods across the street from their home, he sat on the couch with Lindsay.

The entire family was tense, and when Lindsay said something about a medication Chris was taking that she knew was scary, he reacted angrily.

"I don't have to tell you what I'm doing, or keep you updated!"

"Okay, Dad. Okay."

Lindsay felt him separate from her.

—★—

Chris's agitation stewed. He'd shared the tone of the email he'd sent to the college with his parents, which detailed his extensive history of military and law enforcement service, his PTSD, cancer, therapies, and battle with alcoholism.

Brent believed the response Chris received pushed him over yet another edge. He learned that he would need to stand before the board for a review, and that mentally messed him up good.

A cold rain began to fall outside. It was now midday, on Tuesday, December 6th, 2022, and both Brent and Paula were desperately reminding Chris over the phone not to harm himself. That they, his brothers, Tracy, and their daughters' lives would never be the same without him.

He promised he would never do anything to hurt his girls.

That was around 4 p.m.

CHAPTER TWENTY-EIGHT
LAST CALLS

The chaos inside the AuCoin house in Wilton as afternoon passed into early evening was palpable. Tracy was still hopeful Chris would be allowed back into the master's program, but he moved from room to room, kicking up turbulence in his wake. Lindsay also came down with a stomach bug, called out of work, and cancelled plans to see a concert that night. She remained in her room. Bethany took charge in the way she often did, offering to drive Chris to an AA meeting.

"I'll take you, Dad. Let's go. I got you. Let's get into the car and go."

Chris was hesitant, but Bethany insisted.

"Fine, fine. Okay. But can we stop at the Market Basket?" he asked.

Bethany looked at him but nodded. She was strategic as she chose a parking spot and remained in the car. From that vantage point she faced the long panel of windows to track Chris's movements as he walked through the gliding doors. She watched him turn left without breaking stride, as though he had a pre-determined aisle or product in his mind.

She rolled her mouth when her father's frame disappeared from the large rectangular windows near the carts and registers and entered a portion of the large building with no windows. Where the liquor store was.

A few minutes ticked by. Bethany felt that nervous spin in her stomach, the one every AuCoin daughter associated with Chris and his drinking. She watched him re-emerge through the Market Basket windows again and then exit the doors the same way he'd gone in.

"Hey, let's go," he told her once he'd returned to the car. But Bethany knew this routine. Somewhere, under her father's coat, in a pocket, beneath the belt on his pants, he'd stashed a bottle. She watched his face change, as it did every time he was guilty. She knew right then he was hiding alcohol.

"Give me the bottle, Dad."

"What bottle? I don't have a bottle."

Chris offered some resistance, but his daughter refused to let it pass.

"Dad, give me the bottle," she told him.

From beneath the layers of his clothes, Chris produced that signature brown paper bag they were accustomed to him carrying and handed it over.

"Please don't tell Mom, Nana, and Pepe," he requested. His wife and parents, who were already fearing another relapse.

Bethany drove from the Market Basket to the location where the AA meeting would be. She put the car in park and looked at Chris. Tried to smile.

"Bye, Dad. I'll see you after."

Bethany watched Chris enter the building, but he was also watching her. When she drove away, Chris left, walked to a nearby gas station and bought himself another bottle. It was Lindsay who alerted her, because as usual, she was tracking him.

And then the texts started.

Chris wanted to meet Tracy to discuss his new plan to leave New Hampshire and head west on foot. He wanted to walk and told his family he was leaving. Right then and there.

Chris's texts to Tracy asked her to join him at a restaurant near the AA location. He'd asked Bethany not to tell Tracy he'd been drinking, but she wanted her mom to know, in case he tried to contact her and sounded off.

Tracy called Bethany when Chris asked to meet her at a restaurant. While she hated to put her daughter in that position, Tracy felt it best to be transparent in case things got tense.

Bethany offered to stay with Tracy and was used to softening the interactions between them when her father was intoxicated. That night was particularly perilous. Chris was angry. She wanted to mitigate what she could by being there with her parents.

Bethany also had the presence of mind to return to the AA meeting and ask Chris's sponsor to join her. Often, an outside voice quelled the tension, and Chris trusted this man. She and the sponsor walked in together, while Tracy waited outside. Bethany didn't want to bring Tracy in until she felt it was okay for her to join. That took some time. Right away she and Chris's sponsor saw him at the bar.

And he was not happy to see them.

His shoulders hunched as they approached. With one drink before him, and who knew how many had come before that, he told his sponsor, "I really wish you weren't doing this.'"

Chris's sponsor tried every tactic to turn the heat down on Chris's simmering negativity. He applied the right words around the correct messaging, but Chris was in a rapid, multifactorial emotional skid. When the sponsor left the bar, it got worse. Tracy joined them and tried to gently greet Chris. He turned back toward Bethany.

"Listen," he said to her. "I want you in charge of the money. Not Mom. You. Understand?"

Whenever Chris was drinking, a distrust in Tracy was revealed. He didn't believe she had his astute financial judgement and was already irritated with Tracy in general.

As Chris kept drinking, the conversation grew more emotional and unproductive.

"I need you in charge, Bethany," Chris told her again. "You, not your mom. It must be you."

"All right, Dad. Okay. Let's talk some more."

But at that point, Tracy had to go. It pained Bethany to listen to her father's rants, and she herself needed it to stop. She convinced Tracy to leave them at the bar and go home.

"I'll sit with him," she told her. "Please go home, Mom."

They sat there, father and daughter side by side, for some time.

"Let's get some food," she suggested. "I'm hungry. You hungry, Dad? Okay, let's order."

She'd tried to talk about other things, get Chris to eat, and stop drinking.

Finally, he was ready to go home. Bethany looked him in the eye and told him he had to promise her to be cool.

"Dad, promise me you won't escalate or be mean. Let's watch a movie and just rest when we get home. Okay?"

He nodded. "I promise," Chris told her.

Back in the car, Chris turned nostalgic and wistful. "Hey, you remember that time when…" he went on, recalling memories from years ago, a vacation, hike, tossing the ball on the beach, walking the dogs, singing next to a campfire. The pieces of life that had made Chris the happiest. When he was with his girls, feeling like himself, and allowing the joy of togetherness to pass through the plaster cast of his heaviest burdens.

U2 was on the radio. "Ahh, I love this song."

With Or Without You, wafted through the front seat.

"Can we just wait a minute, please."

Chris put his head against the back of the seat and closed his eyes. They sat there in the driveway until the song had played through. Bethany gave her father time and when they got inside, she turned the TV on.

"Come on, Dad. Let's watch a movie."

Chris had other ideas.

—★—

Tracy knew Chris was very drunk. She stayed away from him when he and Bethany got home.

Earlier that day, another troublesome email had arrived, alerting Chris his appeal to get his license back following his highway arrest in New York had been denied. Because of the conviction in that state, his license remained suspended. Between that and the email from the master's program, Tracy had watched Chris decline. He was clearly distraught, and now heavily intoxicated.

He became a supercell of conditions all spinning around at once like winds changing speed and direction as they dropped through the atmosphere. The emails, humiliation, failures, and relapses, all combined like a powerful updraft that rotated through logic and sensibility. And whenever Chris was drunk, the storm was at its fiercest.

"I'm leaving," he announced to them. "Going out west."

By then, Lindsay was out of her room and trying to salvage the night before it got even scarier. While Chris had popped into her room to ask how she was feeling, she knew he was off. Then, the familiar sounds of fighting reached her. Chris and Tracy, downstairs. He was coming at her. Tracy was never combative in turn, but Lindsay heard it getting bad.

Chris climbed up the stairs, and then back down, gathering equipment from other floors in their house and packing contents into a backpack.

"Dad," Lindsay started as she and Bethany stood in the kitchen with him. "Let's just stay here for a while and talk about it."

As two of his daughters pleaded with Chris not to leave, the icy rain outside pelted at the roof and windows. An unnerving rhythm of eerie knocks and pings that created a backbeat of constant noise.

"Okay, okay," he'd say as those prevailing winds in his mind tacked and came about. "Okay, I'm still going out west, but not tonight. I'll leave tomorrow."

Bethany watched her sister work. Lindsay, the tactical comforter, always trying to calm their father. Get him to stay.

But then Chris would collect more items, climb up and down the stairs to retrieve supplies. Volatile and unsteady. Determined and then unsure. Tracy determined it wasn't safe for her in the house that night and was going to leave. Other times when Chris was agitated, Lindsay was able to get him to go to bed and then Tracy would return to the house after that. As she watched Chris gathering items from all floors of the house and packing his backpack, she was trying to stay out of his way.

As Lindsay tried to keep Chris home that night, he'd change his mind again, suddenly furious and frenetically determined.

"No, no, no. I'm leaving now. I'm leaving!"

—★—

Over the course of that night, a smattering of texts went out from Chris.

When Chris Vetter's phone showed a message from Chris, he opened it right away. **Hey pal, thank you for always being there with me, standing next to me, being the next level of leadership in state police. I want you to know I love you.**

Concerned, Vetter called Chris, who picked up. He was drunk. There was noise in the background.

"Hey, man. What's up?" Vetter asked.

They talked about striper fishing, and each committed to going out together soon. But when Vetter hung up, he ruminated on what he'd just heard.

"He's in a bad way," he told his wife. "Chris isn't okay."

Kevin Duffy also received a text from Chris as he was sitting on his couch that night. **Hey, man, you're a good guy. My close friend.**

What the hell was that? He tried to call Chris. He didn't pick up.

Sean Haggerty, who'd always been there to hoist Chris back up, insisted all his mistakes could be remedied, and forced his friend to believe that he had so much more to do, felt those winds shifting direction that night. He had tried to center Chris back into the belief that he could still do all the things he was planning to do.

"All the counseling you'll do, Chris," Sean told him. "You're going to help so many people."

But Chris would call Sean from a bar, as he did that night, drunk on booze and self-loathing. He'd tell him how he'd messed up again. That he was sorry. That night, he refused to tell Sean where he was. Where he offered to come get him, Chris told him no.

"I'm good, all set."

Sean hung up and then worried himself into an uneasy sleep.

Phil Smith had last heard from Chris that weekend, when he'd declined to join him at his house for a Christmas party he held every year to support Toys for Tots. Chris was going to come, and bring his girls, but called Phil the day of and told him he'd had a rough week.

Phil wished he'd read between the lines. A tough week in Chris's life was different. He wished he'd gone to get him. Take him flying. Carried him into the clouds so Chris could tell him what was on his mind.

—★—

Nate answered his phone as his big brother called. It was getting late.

"Hey, where are you?" he asked Chris.

"Never mind that," Chris told him.

He told Nate how he'd always loved him, and that he was sorry.

"Chris, woah, woah, where are you? Let me come see you!"

"See you soon, Nate."

And that was all.

CHAPTER TWENTY-NINE
DEVIATION

Chris had his camping and cold weather gear together. He'd done this so often Tracy and the girls didn't know what to do, telling themselves and each other that he would be fine, they'd been there before, and if they called the police, it would make it worse.

Bethany was at a loss. Lindsay had tried to convince Chris not to leave that night, but he'd disappeared into the woods so many times before, she had to accept that she couldn't prevent him from doing what he wanted to do.

Chris's gun locker was on the third floor of their house, and he was the only one who had the key. He had always kept his service revolver unloaded in the closet with his uniforms. He was very safe with guns and kept his rifle in his cruiser, not a *gun guy,* as Tracy put it.

Chris had gone through a doomsday planning period that summer, and though she didn't consider him suicidal that night—compared to so many nights before—Tracy was always scared that any time Chris was armed and his family or police intervened during a relapse or crisis, a safe outcome for all could not be guaranteed. If Chris was able to get into that gun locker, and he'd stored something inside of it, Brent, Chad, Paula, Tracy, any of them could be at risk. Chris was so cunning, so skilled. Tracy didn't yet know that Chris had gotten an old pistol back from his father. No one could have known if he was hiding a weapon somewhere in his backpack.

As Chris headed toward the door, loaded with survival gear and some level of intoxication, Lindsay attempted a final appeal.

"Dad, please. You can't go out there tonight. It's raining. It's winter!"

He turned and faced her, the daughter who'd hiked the White Mountains of New Hampshire just as he had.

"I'm not like you," he hissed at her. "I know how to hike."

As he left, she noticed his phone. Grabbing it, and a portable charger, she ran down the street after him.

"Dad! Wait!"

Chris turned back.

"Here, please take this." Lindsay handed him both the phone and charger and gave him a hug. "Charge your phone, Dad."

When she called him later to test that he'd answer and his phone was charged, Chris picked up.

"Dad, are you good?" Lindsay asked.

"I'm good," he told her.

"You're not going to hurt yourself, right?"

"No. I would never. I'll be okay."

But Chris would call them soon after. He was angry and rambled on. Something he had said to Tracy just before he'd left the house was chilling in a way she'd never heard from him before.

"If you call anybody, I'll find you," he told her. "There is nowhere you can go where I can't find you."

—★—

Chris also picked up a call from his mother as he walked out of his driveway.

"Chris, please. Go home. It's awful outside. You should just go home."

"Mom, I'll be okay. I need to leave. Don't worry about me."

When he hung up, Paula wondered if that new conviction she'd detected in his voice was a belief they'd all be better without him and the burden his life had become.

—★—

Bethany hated guns. While she recalled arguing with her father like trying to reason with a brick wall, he had told her he wasn't bringing any with him.

"I want my guns, but figured you'd call the cops," Chris told her. "I'm not bringing them."

She sat with Lindsay and Tracy for a while. Her older sister, Kelsey, had moved out and for her own wellness, wasn't as involved as they were in their father's difficulties.

Bethany considered herself the most skilled of her sisters in separating the worry, but that night, she didn't feel safe with her father.

But Lindsay loved him so much and kept tracking him.

When Brent and Chad arrived at their house ready to hike into the woods and power lines to find Chris, they counted the guns in the locker to be sure they were all accounted for.

And then realized one was missing.

—★—

Chad had seen it before, so many times. When Chris was drenched in anger and vodka, he was scary. He and his father were out in the woods, it was raining, visibility was poor. Chad figured his brother was burrowing himself somewhere out there near the power lines, and he coordinated regular calls between Chris and Paula. They were forceful. Intense.

Once, Chris called Brent who put him on speakerphone so Chad could hear.

"If you have anything you have to say, this is the last time you're going to hear from me," Chris told them.

Chad watched his father get defensive, frustrated. While they tracked Chris, and he hung up the phone, his location jumped again. As Chad crunched through wet brush and felt his feet tingle with cold, he ran back through the scenarios they'd discussed back at the house. How Chris had done this before. How he'd probably sleep it off in the woods. How he'd taken all his gear and would be fine. But that nagging thought was creeping up the back of Chad's neck. Ruthlessly present out there in the dank, empty nothingness of space and hollows.

Even if they came upon him out there, Chad feared Chris would think we were cops and shoot. Or that he would beat up their father. His behavior that night hinted at all sorts of possibilities.

At midnight, Chris called Paula who was alone in Jaffrey, desperate for information and clinging to a series of facts she repeated to herself.

He's well trained. He grew up in the woods. Chris never disobeyed authority. If anyone found him, he'd give himself up.

Even as she spoke all of that out loud, Paula fell between the strangest quiet she'd ever experienced, and a roar so loud she pressed her hands over her ears to lock it out.

As December 6th came to an end, Chris called his mom one last time. When he begged her to release him, to let him go… finally, after so many years of hell, he needed it from her the most.

"Mom, please! Listen to me. Release me, Mom. Please release me."

She had to make him stop.

"I release you, Chris. I release you… but… Chris—"

"Goodbye, Mom."

Chris had hung up.

—★—

Lindsay figured Chris's phone battery had died. He'd stopped responding and his last known location was frozen in place. Her stomach, still sour from the virus, and her head heavy with misgivings and woe, she tried to close her eyes and hold onto that same faith that had brought her father home all those times before.

He'll be okay, she told herself. *He's going to be just fine.*

She'd always been able to feel her father's presence, but that night she detected a deviation, an alteration in how her heart and spirit had always acknowledged his on their shared plane.

CHAPTER THIRTY
DIVINE

Daybreak. December 7th, 2022. An empty beer can. A Gatorade bottle. A hat. One glove. Chad followed a path of Chris's belongings and asked himself each time he located an item, *If I were Chris, where would I go?*

He would go on to believe that had been a divine order he was meant to follow. He retraced his steps through the brush from the night before, and then got lost on the trail about two-hundred feet in.

He stopped and looked around. Out of the corner of his eye, Chad noted how something seemed odd. He peered through a hole in the laurel and found his brother.

Chris's face was white, and at first, Chad couldn't tell if he was hurt. He walked up and talked to him, got closer into the mountain laurel. And then he saw.

A small stream of blood had flowed from Chris's ear, nose, and mouth.

Chad stayed still, not wanting to get too close. He still worried how that could spook Chris.

In those agonizing first several seconds, Chad felt suspended in a surreal disbelief, and as he processed what he was looking at, he began to understand what it truly meant. Chris's life had ended. What he was staring at was just the vessel he'd left behind.

—★—

Nate had called his parents, and they'd filled him in, explaining how Brent and Chad were out all night. Chris was volatile again. In the woods, somewhere, they couldn't find him.

He drove himself to the entry point across from Chris's house, and hiked in. About a mile up through the power lines, he found Chad. A cop was already there.

"Is he dead?"

"Yes."

Nate followed the hole through the laurel and knelt at Chris's feet. He held onto his leg and prayed for his brother. It was quiet, and in that stillness, the two brothers knew there was hard news to deliver.

Chad was first, with Nate just behind him as they walked back to where their parents waited. Their eyes, expectant and tortured.

Nate felt the heat of their stare. In that moment, Brent and Paula were still floating between a tiny bit of hope, and a ton of fear. As he got closer to them, Chad was already there. He would be the son who told them.

"He's gone."

Brent and Paula broke down.

Chad and Nate tried to catch them as they fell.

—★—

The brain often dipped into a protective numbness during profoundly catastrophic moments, but Nate remembered what it felt like to know it was his duty to take care of Chris one final time. While Chad and his parents returned to Jaffrey and stayed there, Nate came back for Chris.

He met with two Wilton police officers, and by then the state coroner was there. Then, three troopers showed up, the medical examiner, everyone knew Chris and felt the tremendous pain of his loss.

Nate waited with them as Chris was removed from the woods and loaded into the hearse. More state troopers arrived to escort his brother to the funeral home.

It was a long ride home. As Nate rounded the corner, he called his parents.

"Chris is on his way back to Jaffrey."

The miles and towns faded into each other. The dulled sound of Nate's tires on the highway, the only noise he heard. As he approached the bridge in Jaffrey that spanned the Contoocook River, Nate squinted. There, beneath the light posts, he saw two figures. Two familiar looking, shattered figures who bent around each other, as though one could not stand without the other's fortification.

Brent and Paula were on the bridge, waiting for Chris to come through. The very same bridge that, years before, they'd been warned about. Sister L, at Saint Patrick School, making the contemptible claim that Chris could wind up a future *bridge sitter*, a slur in their town that meant a person had no worth, no value in life.

They stood as strong and straight as they could when Chris passed over the bridge with all the vibrancy he'd earned in life forever intact. A war veteran. The Commander of the New Hampshire State Police SWAT Team. A State Police Major. A husband. A father. A brother and friend.

A beloved son.

Brent used the remaining fragments of strength he had left to lift his arm, angle his hand, and salute his son as the hearse pulled away.

—★—

In Concord, New Hampshire, that morning, a scheduled command staff meeting was getting underway. Chris Vetter entered the building and greeted colleagues around the room. He noticed not all the state police captains and majors were there yet. His phone chimed.

"Hey, get outside. Parking lot. Immediately."

Sean Haggerty had summoned Vetter outside, he practically ran.

Sean had pulled in for the commanders meeting after Vetter. A group of about five to eight command staff members were gathered. One of them came up to his car and told Sean what had happened. As he looked down at his phone, he saw the last call had been from Chris.

Vetter saw them there in the parking lot. He saw Sean. Felt blurry, a bit manic. Unsure of what was going on.

"What's happening?" he asked. "What?"

"Chris killed himself last night."

Vetter dropped to his knees. "But, how? I talked to Chris last night!"

Next, Vetter called Kevin Duffy. They compared the texts and calls many of them had received from Chris the night before.

"It was his final goodbye," Kevin said. Chris hadn't wanted to go without telling each of them how much he'd cared.

Kevin Sullivan was at his desk at work, juggling an exceedingly busy morning with deadlines, clients, and reports all due. His phone lit up. Nate AuCoin was calling. Before he picked up, he was already altering that schedule to make room for Chris. Because that's what brothers did and if Nate needed him to jump in on something, he would drop everything on his calendar and go.

Nate didn't provide specifics, and Kevin didn't ask. His world crashed that day. He stayed at work for a while longer. A co-worker came and sat with him.

"Go home, Sully."

He called Buddy and spent some time on the phone with him.

—★—

Buddy Hackett had a tradition whenever he lost a friend. He kept a bottle of Jameson in his house and did a shot in their honor. But, by 2022, he'd been sober long enough to not do that when Chris died. He didn't take a shot, but did say to himself, *great, he just ruined Pearl Harbor Day for me.*

Chris had never told Buddy why he struggled, and never indicated he was suicidal. But whenever Chris fell, Buddy's hand went out to save him. Time and time again. He would have come if Chris had called. They all would have surged in, if only Chris had asked them to. Buddy reasoned that Chris faced challenges he couldn't fix, though maintained that warrior mentality because a man like that could never be known as soft.

Part of Buddy believed what happened to Chris may have been chemical, some imbalance triggered during cancer. All the PTSD. All the drinking. Maybe even the gunk they'd walked through and breathed in during Operation Desert Storm. He thought of the times Chris and Brent came by his gun shop, one not that long before, that now established a terminal link between them that was never to be erased. The gun Chris had used was the one they'd bought from him.

He felt some guilt over that.

When Brent asked Buddy to speak at Chris's funeral, he says spirit moved him to do so.

The church was filled as Nate, Chad, Sully, Mark, Phil and other members of NH SWAT carried Chris in. Many of his closest friends shared private moments with the AuCoin family, to comfort them—even as they needed it back.

It was one of proudest moments of Buddy's life to share the Chris he knew and loved. He told all his best Chris stories and spoke of the young Marine who was the most earnest guy he'd ever met, who had trudged along beside him in combat readiness as part of what Buddy called the speed bump battalion—*no one cared about you,* he'd tell them. *So be stronger. Be smarter. Be like Chris when you can.*

Frigid air followed them to the gravesite, where Chris would remain forever.

His family, stoic. His friends, huddled together against the chill. His SWAT brothers, shoulder to shoulder.

Mark Hall was the last person to leave the casket.

While there was much said about Chris on the day of his funeral, everyone who loved him still talks at length about him. As often as possible, they share his triumphs, and his disease. Determined to make his life matter.

As Buddy put it, "We all die twice. Our bodies will die first, and then a second time when we're forgotten."

CHAPTER THIRTY-ONE
MASS CAUSATION

To go by legal terms, the word causation refers to that specific relationship between the cause of an event, and the effect or action that followed it. An act or process that would happen and then produce a result. In other words, the thing that caused all the other things to transpire.

Chris's suicide in the woods across the street from his home was a noted incident in the history of New Hampshire law enforcement, and on paper, the causation was subjective, especially for well-meaning strangers who read the impressive obituary, and saw the accompanying picture of Chris, so stern and proud, in his green state police uniform. *That's so sad,* they'd say to each other over coffee or dinner. *I'm so sorry to hear that.* A perfectly respectable response, or effect, to the thing that had happened. To Chris's death.

But the causation elsewhere was seismic.

For Mark Hall, it brought a wonderment he analyzed until a theory he could apply enough reason to, had emerged.

"Other guys would say, 'oh, I talked to Chris,' but I'd wonder why he wasn't talking to me," Mark said. "As things had progressed with Chris, and he declined with alcohol, left the job, I'd reach out to him, text him that I was thinking of him."

What Mark wanted most was for Chris to know he was a good man, that what had happened to him didn't define him.

"What I think is our relationship was different. That Chris knew how much of a mentor he was for me, how much I looked up to him, and he was protecting me. He didn't want to disappoint me with how he was."

Mark also considered that Chris didn't think state police, writ large, wanted to have anything to do with him.

"Chris used to joke with me about how much he knew I loved him and aspired to be like him. He'd say, 'Mark, you're good for my ego.'"

Regardless of the stories that would filter down to Mark as he rose to his current position as Colonel--the role Chris had once considered himself potentially worthy to hold--Mark never doubted Chris would beat it. Whatever *it* was to him.

"I knew he was hurting, but I always prayed Chris would find peace. It just shows you that nobody's immune."

Mark credited Chris, his finest mentor in law enforcement, with instilling in him that impeccable ethos and pride, a quiet competence that made everyone around him better.

"Chris gave everything of himself to us. We need to learn from that and carry it on. It's important to me. Chris is still alive in our organization, we talk about him, we honor him, the good times, and all the things he said to us. It did not end for him as he'd envisioned, but that will never take away from what we gave."

Because of Chris, there are interventions for law enforcement and first responders that either didn't exist just a few years ago or weren't nearly as robust as they are now.

"SWAT now has a good peer and mental health awareness," Mark said. "I've talked to leaders all across the country about it. Police departments across the nation, and New Hampshire is doing it right." Mark called the peer unit, excellent, and plugged in for everybody all the time.

"It's part of the culture now. You no longer feel stigmatized if you go talk to peers and let someone know if you see someone struggling."

As Mark logged over thirty years in his job, he said he'll continue doing just that—but he's aware of the factors, if they were to line up for him, that he'd consider when it came time to remove himself, for his own good and that of everyone who followed his leadership.

"I will do this until I can no longer effectively contribute," he stated. What he will do for himself, that no one seemed to have been able to do for Chris.

"It's hard to look back and think why. Why couldn't we have done this for Chris?"

—★—

Both of Chris Vetter's sons became state troopers, and he was very proud of that. He liked to think most of what he learned from Chris had imprinted onto his own boys through him.

"When I first met Chris, there was an instantaneous feeling that he was the single most professional man I'd ever know. My sons know all about Chris. My version of Chris. I could talk about Chris all day long."

Often, when thoughts of Chris rushed in and Vetter second guessed what he could have done differently, he'd force himself to remember all the other moments. When Chris would text him at 5 am on a holiday morning. **Hey, pal, enjoy the day with your family.**

Little things. Monumental things. Chris had been by his side for them all.

When Vetter and Chris were just starting out, there wasn't room for emotion or any outward expression of feeling overwhelmed. He's glad that's changing.

"We were young. We'd see things, and there was no plan to deal with incidents on the job. It's vastly different now, there's constant reach out and resources available to them. And I'm there for my sons. I will always be there for my sons, doing this job. By the time anyone really knew about

Chris, he was so far down the road, the course was set, and he was in a spiral. We tried. It wasn't enough."

—★—

"Chris would never tell anyone. Never talked out of some mutual respect for each other."

Kevin Duffy believed that Chris carried parts of everything he'd ever experienced, and all of that became too heavy.

"You don't realize you're carrying it until you're out from under it," he said.

He called the day he handed over his retirement letter at New Hampshire State Police headquarters, affirmation of that.

"I went up to the third floor on Hazen Drive and gave it to the executive major. We had a talk. When I left that building, I felt like I was walking on air."

The relief of handing off that part of his life was singularly unique, as though the rigidness of how he thought, moved, breathed, and planned, had loosened. Suddenly, he could see all the colors around him, and he marveled at how gentrified they'd become.

"I had always tried to be an optimistic person, to try and see the positive with a good attitude and a smile. But once I retired, I'd run into former colleagues and they'd say, 'Wow, you look so happy!' And I'd think, holy shit, I thought I was happy then!"

So, what changed, he asked himself. "I think it's the psychological demeanor. I was suddenly what I hadn't been for an entire career."

But not everyone crawled out from that narrow and stiff sheath.

"Chris literally gave his life for all the good that he did. He lost everything in the process."

—★—

Sean Haggerty says it simply wasn't right or welcomed to share hard emotions. "Early on, it wasn't a thing to talk about yourself. Or, to ask, are you okay? We were such a tight group we'd joke around in the BEAR as we drove out to a warrant, or location. But then a switch turned on and we got to work. We had each other by our side and counted on us all being okay. Of being fine."

In 2013, Sean was at the Boston Marathon when bombs exploded near the finish line. "They did relentlessly check in on me," he said of the peer-to-peer program. "I know it's there now. But it wasn't early on. It wasn't there for Chris at the level he needed. We're on the better side of that now."

If something popped up, Sean knew where to go for support, and called it a good job on the part of the state in moving to that place for troopers. But what should they do when and if it all fails? How can they find a way to see through the protective veneer many of them built to hide away the ache of vulnerability? How could they find a better way to reach the men and women who were silently suffering?

"What do we do when nothing works? How do we look out for all of us, for Chris, when whatever's in place doesn't deliver?"

—★—

The dedication in Kevin Sullivan's dissertation to earn his PhD in counselor education and supervision was to Chris. It read in part: *Without Chris's support and motivation, I would never have been able to decide to begin or continue this research journey.*

"In Chris and my own research and work, I believe post traumatic stress can be overcome." Kevin's life mission, before Chris's death, but especially after, became the other side of PTSD. "To get veterans able to see it. To get them to the other side."

He's one of the foremost experts in New Hampshire on combining services and therapies with law enforcement—to get them proactively seeking help rather than using substances as coping skills.

"We're removing the old school ways," Kevin explained. "To go have a few beers after a bad shift, to now staying together to talk about it. To pray about it."

While he's not yet empirically convinced of the long-term effects of that strategy, Kevin remained hopeful. "I like to think it's solid."

Another change in how mental health was being managed in law enforcement and among veterans was to remove stigmas and normalize it. Kevin saw expectations in newer members just entering the field that were more consistent with the larger community.

"They're coming in and asking about it right away. Will it be available? Before it wasn't mandatory, now we go and learn how to deal with negative emotions, and how we interact with our families. If we don't share our day with them, it's not protecting them by trying to protect them."

The older guard of law enforcement, Kevin said, was leaving.

"More and more every day."

Kevin was proud that Chris was working toward becoming a counselor, but when he reflected upon that time now, he—like everyone who loved Chris—asked himself if he hadn't paid him enough attention. If he'd been too busy with the demands of his own educational pursuit.

"It's that mixture of knowing on a clinical level that I am trained to do my best work, but either couldn't or didn't for Chris."

Kevin also knew as an insider what the industry analysis of Chris was going to be. What that looked like on a granular level when a veteran in the care of the VA died by suicide. How records were examined, case notes reviewed line-by-line, treatment plans deconstructed, and that the entire lot of it was then shared throughout the district.

"We want to find the something. The something that could have been done differently."

—★—

"Chris was my idol growing up," Chad said. Like his big brother, Chad also became a pilot and has had a highly successful career. Though much of his life, he said, was spent resenting the agony and pain Chris was causing him and his family. The time he had to spend away from his wife and children when Brent and Paula called in reinforcements.

"My parents were constantly updating me on Chris. It had made it unbearable for my parents to spend any time with me."

He believed it was the job that made Chris hard. "He'd been the one to teach me how to ski, and scuba. Chris was goofy and fun. So adventurous. He'd take me around in his cruiser and pull people over for no reason."

But those softer edges had turned to iron, Chad thought. "I used to tell him, Chris, your blood is blue, but your heart is black."

For Chad, the process of letting Chris go had begun long before that early morning discovery in the woods.

—★—

Nate believed that we, collectively as human beings, maintained the will to fight even when things were going well, but especially when they went bad. But it sure got harder to do it on your own.

"The problem is, unless the right person can dedicate the rest of their life to helping the person that needs them, is there nothing else that will help them?"

He'd watched Brent and Paula relentlessly pursue facilities, options, analyze legal documents and police reports, and remain committed to Chris even as their own health and wellness were being battered. "They tried to find pieces of something that were good. But Chris wasn't okay. Ever."

When someone got that low, where Nate considered Chris to be most of the time, he wasn't sure there was a fix, because they could never find one. But he has reconciled the exclusive blend of emotion he felt for Chris, as tangled and serrated as it had become.

"The one thing about loss. Life is for the living and anyone that we lose would not want us to be alive but not live."

Nate held regrets but woke up every day trying to lay those aside.

"I'm trying to live for Chris now. And not just live in the fact that he's gone."

—★—

Tracy and Chris's daughters' concept of safety changed throughout Chris's illness, but more so after he was gone.

"When we were younger, I never worried about my safety," Tracy said. "Chris would take care of it. But that morphed into him being the one person I was afraid of."

She called that fear, life changing.

Bethany said it took a long time to lose her dad.

"He was sick for so long," she remembered. "When he passed, it's sad but we can now move on and I know my mom is safe, that nothing bad is going to happen. It's done now."

She expects that sadness for the dad that she lost to be lasting, but Bethany grieved Chris more when he was alive than she does now. Empathy remains in her heart for what her father had been holding.

"I would've loved that guy now, but the guy he turned into, I don't want that in my life."

Lindsay knew her dad never wanted any of them to know how bad it was. How much he'd struggled. That was the hardest part, and when she was scared to go to sleep once her father was gone.

"He's not here. Our rock. My dad always wanted us to have that view of him, that we were all safe with him."

—★—

There's an old saying that went like this: *There really are places in the heart you don't even know exist until you love a child.* And, while there could be many other sayings applied to the life and death of Chris AuCoin, none fit more seamlessly. He was truly loved every moment of his life by his mom and dad.

"We were never terrified for ourselves," Paula said. "It was for Chris. He'd become a force we didn't recognize. We spent ten years of our lives trying to figure out how to prevent a tragedy."

The coiled complications of loving someone so determined to destroy himself, drove them to a level of desperation they still haven't descended from three years later as this book was being written. They were dumbstruck by Chris, awed, worried, devastated—and like a spin cycle washing machine they could never lift the lid on to climb out of, it wound them tighter and drew them farther away from the life they'd planned so carefully to have. Two intelligent, loving parents—not so unlike millions more in the world dealing with similar problems—felt like they were blindfolded and set free into a place they didn't recognize. To figure it out as they went.

"How do you, as a parent, say I'm sorry, Chris. We've had enough. Goodbye. Even if it upset the boys, we couldn't stop. I know they were mad about that, and I can see their side, too, that Chris was wearing us out, and what about them, that it was always Chris getting all the attention," Brent said. "But I would die for any of my boys."

Some studies put thoughts of suicide among parents who have lost children as high as 65%. The grief, so personal and intense a mother or father cannot find a will to go on. Brent became tormented. He saw no solution other than a lasting quiet of his own making.

"If I die the same way Chris did, I would go to where he was."

Brent tried. More than once, to get there.

"I couldn't ever let my guard down," Paula said. "I couldn't grieve myself because I was on watch for Brent."

Brent was saved each time and has begun to work with trusted partners to relieve himself of suicidal ideations. He calls this book part of that.

"It's both painful and healing," Brent said. "Talking about Chris this way lets the steam out of the kettle."

But the wounds wreaked havoc on the healing. The doubts and guilt that spoke the loudest to them both in the middle of the night.

What did we miss? How did this happen? What was Chris telling us that we couldn't hear?

Brent believed women were stronger than men and found some irony in the fact that Chris had fathered three daughters. "Paula can somehow stand stronger than I, she has a lot of grit."

But, in that way, did anyone ever really have a choice? Paula didn't think so. "I can't go down the rabbit hole. I have an entire family to live for."

The AuCoins rescued Chris many times, and their never-give-up approach gave them ten more years together. Even after a decade of hyper-vigilance, near misses, and the darkest night of their lives, there were still days when Chris felt so close to them it seemed he was about to show up in their driveway or text them that he was on his way over to talk about a new idea or project he'd been working on.

"We always felt Chris would make it."

Suicide remains one of the most esoteric and cryptic acts a person can carry out, even as it's studied, analyzed, researched and dissected by generations of scholars and advanced science.

"I think it happens quickly," Paula said. "That something happens inside of you, and you decide it's time. Chris may not have been suicidal when he went into the woods that night but then changed his mind."

With Chris gone, and that motherly curtain she'd built around him lifted away, Paula still felt a permanency between them. From her body and heart, Chris had entered the world. And, after he'd begged her to release him, he'd left it. If she would never learn the answers why Chris did what he did that night, maybe he'd want her to find some peace in that.

Brent and Paula decided to tell Chris's story, in all its wonderful and horrific detail, so that his legacy would go on and changes would be made. So that the process to treat veterans and members of law enforcement could be examined more closely, refined and improved. They hope that someone will read this book, think about Chris, and then recommend it to someone else who may need it. Maybe a veteran like Chris who was battling similar demons, who may hear his voice calling out in these pages.

This book and Chris's memory are left here to become what he'd been working to be: A safe harbor from the storm that raged within, but no one else could see. A push forward to find the help, peace, and a way back to the people who were waiting with all the love his family and friends had held for him.

And also, because what Chris had faith in most when he was far from them, an entire world away, fighting a war with all the courage he could muster, was that one day, he would see them all again. To let them know that if they didn't worry about him, Chris would be just fine.

To tell them one last time, *I'm okay, if you're okay.*

A LETTER FROM MOM TO CHRIS

Dear Son,

I want you to know you were saving lives even before you were born. You saved mine when I was a young woman at 16 who was lost. I desperately needed someone to love unconditionally and to receive love in the same way. You did that for me from the moment you were conceived. You brought a feeling of joy and completeness. I carry that feeling of joy today, grateful to God for allowing me to be your mother, for God taking a chance on me to raise you, nurture you, and love you at such a young age.

You gave me the mother and child bond that I so desperately needed. You were part of me; you grew in my body and will always live in my heart. I tried so desperately to save you from the darkness and pain. I always had hope that you would get to the other side of this pain, I did not expect that the pain would end the way it did. I do understand your pain and why you felt you couldn't bear it any longer.

You saved me but I could not save you.

Rest in peace, my beautiful boy, with my dad, and your grandpa Charlie, who you never had a chance to meet, but always had a spiritual connection with. He was always watching from above, with pride, awaiting the day he would meet you.

I will continue to live my life to honor you through helping others who suffer the way you did and to carry on your legacy of serving others.

Grief is love that has nowhere to go; If only love could have saved you.

Until we meet again, my first-born son,

Your Loving Mom

A LETTER FROM PAULA TO CHRIS CENTERED ON OUR PHONE CALL

My sweet Chris,

There is a moment I go back to more than any other — the last time we talked on the phone. I can still hear your voice. I can still feel the ache behind your words. And I need to speak to you about it, because it has lived in my heart ever since.

You said, "Release me, Mom." Just like that. Quiet. Tired. Almost like a whisper from somewhere deep inside you. I remember freezing for a second, because I didn't understand what you meant. I thought you were overwhelmed, or scared, or caught in one of those waves that had been hitting you so hard.

I thought you needed grounding. Comfort. A mother's reassurance.

So I did what I had always done—I tried to calm you. I told you it was okay. I told you to breathe. I told you we would get through it. I thought you were asking me to help settle your mind, not your soul. I didn't know you were asking for something bigger. I didn't know you were carrying a weight that had become unbearable. I didn't know you were standing at the edge of something I couldn't see.

If I had understood —truly understood—I would have spoken differently. I would have listened with my heart instead of my fear. I would have said: Chris, I love you. I see your pain. I'm not holding you here out of fear—I'm holding you because you're my son. But if you're asking me to let go of the guilt you feel, the shame you carry, the torment that follows you… then yes, my boy, I release you from that. I release you from the burden you think you are. I release you from the lies that tell you you're too broken to be loved. I release you into God's hands, where there is peace I can't give you.

But I didn't know. I didn't know you were saying goodbye in the only way you could. And Chris… I need you to hear this now, from the deepest place in me: I wasn't ignoring you. I wasn't dismissing you. I was loving you the only way I knew how in that moment. I was trying to keep you here. I was trying to keep you safe. I was trying to keep you alive.

No mother is ever prepared for her son to ask for release. No mother is ever ready to imagine what that might mean. But now, with time and tears and prayer, I can say the words I couldn't say then: I release you, my son. Not from my love—that will never end. But from the pain that chased you. From the war that followed you home. From the weight you carried alone.

You are free now. Free in a way you longed for. Free in a way I couldn't understand at the time. And I hold you—not with fear, not with regret—but with a mother's love that has no end and no boundaries.

Until I see you again,

Mom

A MADE-UP CONVERSATION BETWEEN DAD AND CHRIS

Dad:

"Chris… I miss you so much. There are days I still reach for you without thinking. I keep wishing I could have said more— or done more—to help you stay. I just want to talk to you. Even for a moment.

Chris:

"I know. I feel those moments. And I wish I could take your pain away—all of it. I never wanted to leave you with this ache. Not once."

Dad:

"Then why, Chris? Why did it end the way it did? I keep replaying everything… wondering what I missed, what I didn't see. I would have done anything to help you."

Chris:

"I know you would have. You always did more than you'll ever give yourself credit for. You were there for me in ways I couldn't even understand at the time. It wasn't your failure—it was my pain. It was too loud… too heavy… too constant. I wasn't thinking clearly. I wasn't choosing between life and death—I was choosing between pain and silence."

Dad:

"But you weren't a burden. You were never too much. I wish you knew that."

Chris:

"I know that now. I couldn't see it then. The darkness twisted everything. It told me that you would all be better off without my struggles, without my weight, without the version of me I felt trapped inside. But listen to me—really hear this: I was wrong. Not you. Not the family. Me. I was hurting, not thinking. And I never stopped loving you."

Dad:

"I would give anything to go back and hold you through that pain. To make you stay. To show you, you were worth saving."

Chris:

"And I would give anything to come back and let you. But I want you to understand something important: What happened wasn't your responsibility to prevent. You didn't fail me. You loved me—the whole me—even when I couldn't love myself. And that love still matters. It still reaches me. It still carries forward. Don't let my darkest moment become your burden to carry forever."

Dad:

"It's hard, Chris. Some days the grief hits so suddenly I lose my breath. Other days I feel numb. I'm afraid of letting go—like it means losing you again.

Chris:

"You don't have to let go of me. Just the guilt. Just the self-blame. Just the idea that you could have fixed what I never spoke out loud. Hold onto the love. Hold onto the memories. Hold onto the laughter, the stories, the moments that were ours. I am not lost. I am not gone. I'm just… out of sight."

Dad:

"Do you forgive me, Chris? For anything I failed to see, or say, or do?

Chris:

"Mom… Dad… There is nothing to forgive. Nothing. You gave me everything you had. Every bit of strength. Every bit of love. Every bit of hope. The part that broke had nothing to do with you. If anything… I wish you'd forgive yourselves."

Dad:

"I love you, Chris. More than anything. More than these words will ever say.

Chris:

"I love you too. More than my pain ever let me show. More than this world ever let me feel. And that love—yours and mine—is stronger than the night that took me. I'm with you. In the quiet. In the tears. In the sunlight on the trees. In the moments you don't expect. In the ones where you talk to me without realizing it. I'm here. I'm okay now. And I want you to live. *Really* live. For both of us."

A LETTER TO CHRIS FROM MOM AND DAD

Chris,

There are moments when we still expect to hear your footsteps, or your voice calling from the other room, or the sound of your laughter drifting in the way it used to. Even now, we find ourselves turning toward the door as if you might walk through it. The heart remembers things long after the world has changed.

There is not a single day—not one—when you are not with us in some way. Sometimes in memories that make us smile. Sometimes in memories that break us wide open. Sometimes in the quiet moments when we feel you close, almost like you're trying to tell us, "I'm okay."

We wish you could have seen yourself the way we saw you. You had a softness in you, a depth, a sensitivity most people never develop. You were loved beyond words. You were wanted. You were needed. We know life felt heavy for you. Too heavy. Heavier than any parent ever wants to imagine their child carrying. And we're sorry—more than words can ever reach—that the weight pressed on you the way it did.

But Chris… please hear this:

Nothing you faced changed how deeply we loved you.

Nothing you struggled with made you any less our child.

Nothing you felt made us ashamed.

Nothing you went through made you alone.

If love could have lifted you fully out of the darkness, we would have carried you ourselves. A thousand times over. And we still would today.

We carry your story now—not as a wound alone, but as a piece of our heart that grew stronger, deeper, more compassionate because you were here. Because you lived, because you loved, because you mattered.

Your brothers miss you in ways you would never believe.

Your mother carries you in every heartbeat.

Your family still speaks your name with love, not just pain.

And I want you to know something that took us a long time to understand: Your story didn't end the night you left this world. It continues in us—in the strength we've found, in the love we've rediscovered, in the way we hold each other tighter, in how we honor you by trying to live with the gentleness you deserved.

Chris, our child, our heart—we hope you have found the peace you were searching for. We hope you feel light, unburdened, whole. And we hope you know this one truth that time cannot erase:

We love you.

We will always love you.

And we will carry you with us for as long as we have breath.

Love,

Mom and Dad

A LETTER TO OUR VETERANS AND FIRST RESPONDERS WHO LOST THEIR BATTLE TO SUICIDE

We are writing this to you, not in judgment, but in love.

The world has often misunderstood the truth about your deaths. Too many have called it selfish. Too many have assumed you didn't care enough to stay. But we know better. Your families know better. Your brothers and sisters in service know better. And the truth, revealed through your stories—through Chris's story, through thousands like his—is this:

You did not die because you didn't love your families. You died because you loved them so deeply you believed they deserved a burden-free version of you. This terrible lie—this belief that your loved ones would be "better off without you"—is not selfishness. It is a symptom of profound suffering. Your stories reveal what the research confirms: what psychologists call perceived burdensomeness, a cruel distortion created by PTSD, trauma, chronic pain, and relentless emotional weight.

It is the same torment seen in King David's anguish: "My heart is in anguish within me… horror has overwhelmed me."

It is the same cry uttered by the prophet Elijah: "I have had enough, Lord. Take my life."

Your suffering was ancient.

Your courage was immeasurable.

You spent your lives protecting others.

You stood in danger so others could live.

You carried memories, images, pain, and guilt most humans will never see—not even in their nightmares. And when the battles turned inward—when nightmares invaded daylight, when medications piled to 31 pills a day, as with our son Chris, when hope felt far away and help felt out of reach—you were not abandoning us. You were trying to escape a pain that had become unbearable, unending, and inescapable.

Many of you, like Chris, were failed by systems that should have protected you—systems that over-medicated, under-listened, dismissed your cries, and sent you home with nothing more than a bottle and a prayer.

You fought for your families.

You fought for your communities.

You fought for strangers.

And you fought—quietly, painfully—for yourselves.

Your final act was not a betrayal. It was the tragic end of a battle you had been fighting alone for far too long. We want you to hear this now, with the dignity you deserve:

You were not selfish.

You were wounded.

You were exhausted.

You were loved.

And you still are.

Your families carry your story forward not in shame, but in honor—telling the truth that suicide is not moral failure, not weakness, not lack of love, but the devastating result of invisible wounds that were never properly treated, never fully understood. You did not die in disgrace. You died from injuries inflicted long before the world ever knew you were hurting.

You are heroes—not because of how you died, but because of how you lived: with courage, with loyalty, with sacrifice, and with love that asked for nothing in return. Your story is now our mission—a call to action to demand better care, integrated healing, and systems that see the human behind the uniform. And to every one of you—veterans, police officers, firefighters, EMTs, corrections officers, dispatchers— we say this:

You mattered.

Your life had meaning.

Your struggle had purpose.

Your death was not your fault.

We honor you.

We remember you.

We fight for the ones still here because of you.

And we will tell the world the truth: Suicide is not selfish. Silence is deadly. Compassion is the cure. With love, reverence, and unending gratitude.

For every life lived in service.

For every battle fought in silence.

For every warrior who deserved more time.

May you finally know the peace you were searching for all along.

God Bless our men and women who serve God, our Country and our neighbors!

With Love,

Brent and Paula AuCoin

RESOURCES AND REFLECTIONS

Over the course of a decade, Chris AuCoin was either hospitalized or in treatment at over two dozen facilities up and down the East Coast. Many of those preceding incidents are not chronicled in this book, though they are as equally dramatic and emotional as the ones that are. They include suicidal episodes, when Chris tried to run into oncoming traffic, or was found unresponsive in a park, experienced almost total muscle breakdown, lost cognition during electric shock treatment, was intubated, and left his family notes alerting them of his intention to leave this world. At times, the events were back-to-back, while others were separated by weeks or months, when Chris was able to demonstrate more of a lasting commitment to sobriety, therapy in many forms, and recovery.

When Chris died, every person who participated in this book broke down in shock and sadness, but there are so many more impacted by the magnitude of his loss. Not only was Chris renowned across New Hampshire law enforcement circles, but he was also the perceived strongest among them, unbreakable in body and spirit. But, of course, he was not.

To a lifelong man of the law, as Dr. David Goldstein is, Chris's story is hellish, but hardly unique. Therein lies the dual purpose of Dr. Goldstein's life: Law enforcement, and the psychology of being an imperfect human in that line of work.

"Part of our identity is being a cop," Dr. Goldstein explains. "And I cry alone."

Decades ago, the work was insular, and officers were expected to shoulder it mostly alone. Dr. Goldstein calls that an overarching structural unwillingness to engage in helping officers after an event. When he was coming up as a cop in Massachusetts during the 1970s, developing his personality as both an intellectual and member of law enforcement, Dr. Goldstein carved out a path to functionally join the two disciplines: mental health and policing the streets. At first, it happened when no one was looking. Dr. Goldstein would get a call and head out for a meeting in the dark of night and in plain clothes.

"Hey, we got trouble," someone would tell him. "I need to bring you in on something."

At one or two o'clock in the morning, Dr. Goldstein would arrange a clandestine meeting at a 24-hour Dunkin' Donuts. No one had to know. He'd sit across from someone who'd seen something bad and try to unravel the thread before it got impossibly tight and choked out the air.

Word began to spread. There was no shame in talking to Dr. Goldstein. His late-night meetings went on for many years, even as he grew a family, earned his MS in public health and a doctorate in psychology/sociology, moved to New Hampshire, joined the ranks with state police, and met Chris AuCoin.

"He always called me sir," Dr. Goldstein says of Chris. Both men knew the arduous nature of NHSP SWAT, and because they were close in that way, Chris never approached Dr. Goldstein.

"I think part of that may have been that he was embarrassed. I've seen that a lot in cops."

Did Chris give off signs? "No. And I ask myself why I didn't see this."

But then again, even with his exclusive background in both police work and mental health, no one ever told him.

"No one came to me about Chris AuCoin. Even now, when members of state police retire, they're off the grid and done. They don't call me, even if they need to talk. Even if they're in trouble. They still bleed green, the color of the uniform."

Consider the numbers. If there are roughly only nine-hundred-thousand police officers working the entire country's cities and towns, the inevitability of PTS, or post-traumatic stress, is all but set in stone.

"These are the men and women who protect us all, doing a phenomenal job, so the PTSD for them is almost normalized." But in that, Dr. Goldstein notes the conflict.

"Chris, in telling someone he has an issue, it often translates into 'help me' but being human, with pathways in our brains that don't line up, we'll do our best to thwart that, but we don't know how to fix that."

And to treat mental illness, Dr. Goldstein points to one non-negotiable.

"You have to get rid of the booze!"

Which is something Chris never could sustain. There's also self-reporting intelligence that Dr. Goldstein examines from law enforcement spouses. Forty percent of them admit to at least one incident of domestic violence.

"We can't ignore that," Dr. Goldstein says.

At times, he's been compelled to report his own colleagues because of statements their wives have given. Part of that is what he attributes to the systemic failure of the system. Of its poor history of relapse, loss of connection or break in the clinical relationship, and what he describes as a self-imposed method of getting better. And while there needs to be some responsibility on that person to seek and accept help, the law enforcement community must be there if someone knocks on the door. They must answer the call and be prepared for whatever, and whoever, is on the other side, and then maintain that link between them forever.

"The bosses, they're the ones who have to weigh in, accept it," Dr. Goldstein says. "A lot of bosses in my time had the 'suck it up buttercup' attitude. It's still out there, not as prominent as it was, but it's a defense mechanism on their part to do their job and not get fired." He calls that very sad.

But what does it take to remove a defense mechanism that is so ingrained it might as well be impenetrable? Dr. Goldstein puts Chris on the higher end of a bell curve, and if many in law enforcement are somewhere on that curve, he was extreme. Chris lands there for several reasons, including one that may seem odd given how physically formidable he was.

"Stage 4 level illness is physical," Dr. Goldstein explains. "You're going to die, waste away. Alcohol makes it so much easier to kill yourself. All suicides, as they're investigated, the odor comes up in the autopsy, wafts right out of the body. It's a smell you don't forget."

He believes Chris's alcoholic body was failing him in many ways, but most he likely couldn't recognize. If he could talk to Chris, he'd tell him the straight facts: that stress and substance abuse to manage it will kill men like him more than knives and guns ever could. He'd tell Chris how it would destroy his family and break him down. He'd explain how the average citizen might experience three or four critical incidents in a lifetime, but the average cop sees upwards of eight hundred. If Chris had asked Dr. Goldstein what to do with that, he would have provided the boundaries for Chris to experience what he needed to and then let him decompress and rest. And he'd tell Chris that no matter what, he'd always be there.

The AuCoin family did exactly that. And then some.

"The pain suicidal people feel, I'd rather have a compound fracture," Dr. Goldstein adds. "It is interminable and constant. A lot of us can't appreciate that level of pain, it's a psychic pain that outweighs physical pain. They're just trying to alleviate the pain. Chris was doing that. Drinking, anger, violence. All expressions of pain."

Much has changed in the years since Chris left this world.

"We have the Southern New Hampshire Critical Incident Stress Management Team. Over a dozen police departments are now involved. We debrief and defuse, sometimes it's individual. Informal. NHSP has a team. But we all need to share resources. We can cross-pollinate."

(https://responderstogethernh.org/regional--state-cism-teams.html)

Dr. Goldstein believes there will always be groupings of the walking wounded among us, and that no matter how hard everyone tries, they may remain stuck. But the helpers must know where to find them, or better, establish a clinical or educational backstop before they're lost.

"My role now is to address wellness. What that looks like. Figure out with our young recruits how to make them listen and buy in."

What Dr. Goldstein and others like him can teach men and women at the earliest point in their careers, before they even know what they're going to do in their lives, may be key in avoiding that bottomless pain. To show them how to reach out. How to talk about what they're feeling.

And how to fix it.

Which is what this book, the AuCoin family, and an expanding village of mental health experts are earnestly trying to figure out.

If we look solely at the numbers, there is an argument that they remain frustratingly stagnant, even as the VA calls its 2025 report (2023 data) one that finds "hopeful" metrics: In 2023, 6,398 Veterans died by suicide, which was 44 fewer deaths than in 2022. According to the report, the 2023 total was lower than 14 of the previous 15 years, which reflects recent momentum in suicide prevention efforts.

(https://news.va.gov/145433/2025-national-veteran-suicide-prevention-report/)

But what happens when one of those 6,398 veterans is your son? Your daughter? Your parent? And will we ever know what that veteran went through, the treatment sought, medication prescribed, or his grueling counseling schedule? What about veterans who never report their symptoms and suffer in silence? How do we reach them, too? Unless you are close to a veteran or law enforcement professional in crisis, the answers are still not as all-encompassing as we need them to be. The AuCoin family exhausted VA resources, private therapy, in-patient detox treatment, medication, and all other methods of care. They did this for over a decade as Chris was catapulting through one harrowing event after another. And still, Chris could not be saved.

But in that tragedy, this family sees a crack wide enough for the light to shine in. His story does not have to be yours, your child's, your neighbor's, or any precious soul in crisis. If we follow the cues and learn, as a nation, how to intervene, circumvent, soothe, support, encourage faith practices, and work through love—the AuCoins believe there is an emerging path back to stability and recovery. The timing is crucial, as Dr. Goldstein notes, because the pervasive attack on the mental health of our country's servicemembers appears to be ensnaring many of them almost immediately upon stepping into uniform.

There are now emerging data markers that suggest PTSD is either being reported more often, or leaching into the next generation of soldiers, and others, at an alarming rate. According to a Yale School of Medicine study released in September of 2025 in the Journal of Clinical Psychiatry: Younger U.S. military veterans are three times more likely to experience post-traumatic stress disorder (PTSD) than their older counterparts, largely due to greater psychological and social challenges, according to a new study led by researchers at Yale School of Medicine and the National Center for PTSD.

(https://www.psychiatrist.com/jcp/identifying-factors-higher-prevalence-posttraumatic-stress-disorder-younger-us-military-veterans/)

Is this battle in the brain the product of a singular traumatic experience for someone at the starting point of her career, or the culmination of many? In this, imagine the police officer who responds to a fatal car crash, a domestic violence incident, a shooting, an injured child, a crime victim—in perpetuity. If that officer develops symptoms of PTSD, was it the injured child that resulted in that diagnosis? The shooting? Or was it the sum of every experience of that officer's career? And at what point would psychological intervention be impactful in preventing a singular symptom from declining into full PTSD, or worse? There may be an opportunity here to balance the data from the Yale School of Medicine, with an FBI examination of law enforcement's magnitude of incidents, or the quantity of perilous memories that even a highly trained person can functionally manage.

(https://leb.fbi.gov/articles/perspective/perspective-the-impact-of-life-experiences-on-police-officers).

In April of 2026, the US Department of Health and Human Services was tasked to tread farther into the vortex of complex and treatment-resistant mental illness, to rapidly expand access and investigate potentially burgeoning medical developments. Health and Human Services wants to accelerate research, approval, and responsible access to promising mental health treatments—including psychedelic therapies like Ibogaine—to better manage the mental health crisis in this country, with a particular focus on veterans. With this so-called Breakthrough Therapy designation, the federal government will endeavor to investigate early evidence and any meaningful improvement over existing options.

(https://www.fda.gov/news-events/press-announcements/fda-accelerates-action-treatments-serious-mental-illness-following-executive-order).

If there is to be a new class of medications soon, benefits outweigh risks, and if they prove to be effective, the concept of right-to-try novel therapies may experience a more rapid clearance to investigational human trials. In this evolving medical landscape, Kevin Sullivan wants another message to be applied.

Kevin F. Sullivan, PhD:

When working with veterans, it is very important to me to watch for the following risk factors for suicide. The risk factors I look for are prior suicide attempts, chronic mental health issues, substance abuse, access to lethal means, recent loss, legal or financial troubles, relationship issues, unemployment, and homelessness. If I were to identify any of these factors when working with a Veteran, I would address it directly with them and try to coordinate care to help resolve that specific issue. In conjunction with looking for risk factors, I also try to determine protective factors such as their access to mental health care, their sense of connectedness to others, their ability to solve problems, their sense of spirituality, their purpose, their physical health, their employment status, and their social and emotional well-being.

My experience has taught me that PTSD is complex, and treatment is relative to the individual. My organization does a terrific job at care coordination and supervision with all cases. Treatments include Psychotherapy, Prolonged Exposure Therapy, Cognitive Processing Therapy, Eye Movement Desensitization and Reprocessing (EMDR), and Group therapy. Moral injury groups have also been successful as well. In addition to mental health treatment is changing lifestyle. Some of those changes include adapting to regular physical activity and improving sleep hygiene, mood, and resilience. Mindfulness, yoga, meditation, or prayer can help regulate stress responses. Social connection and safe, stable environments support recovery and prevent relapses. Any type of reducing or eliminating self-medication, such as alcohol or drug misuse, is crucial, as these can worsen symptoms.

New treatments being considered are ketamine therapy, MDMA-assisted psychotherapy, and neurofeedback. MDMA-assisted psychotherapy has the most robust evidence base.

Ketamine and Esketamine, Psilocybin, LSD, DMT, Ayahuasca, and Ibogaine. A 2025 systematic review concluded that MDMA and ketamine currently have the strongest evidence, while compounds like psilocybin, LSD, ayahuasca, and ibogaine show preliminary but promising results. My main concern is that Veterans will view these treatments as too quick to cure their symptoms. Any of these interventions should be in conjunction with mental health counseling.

I personally received a stellate ganglion block (SGB), which is an injection of a local anesthetic into the neck to decrease pain and block the fight or flight response, which decreases PTSD symptoms.

This procedure still works better with a connection with a mental health provider.

Eric Golnick, Navy Veteran:

Eric Golnick is a Navy veteran, and this is personal for him, as his extensive resume will show. The founder of Deep Current Strategies, Chair of the National Association of Veteran and First Responder Wellness, Co-founder and former CEO, Forge Veteran and First Responder Health, former national security and defense policy advisor, and a congressional and US Senate witness of veteran mental health, substance use, suicide prevention, and access to care, Golnick believes the systems are often too slow when people finally ask for help.

In his own words, this is what he wants readers of this book to know:

The first thing I would want people to understand is that isolation is one of the most dangerous parts of suicide risk.

That does not always mean someone is physically alone. A person can be surrounded by family, coworkers, teammates, and people who love them, and still feel completely cut off. Isolation can look like shame. It can look like silence. It can look like someone believing they are a burden, or that no one could possibly understand what they are carrying.

That is why waiting for someone to "look suicidal" is dangerous. Many people who are struggling are still functioning. They are still going to work, answering calls, making jokes, caring for their families, and showing up for everyone else. From the outside, they may look fine. Inside, they may be in real trouble.

The warning signs are often quieter than people expect. Pulling away. Drinking or using substances more. Sleeping badly. Becoming more agitated or reckless. Losing purpose. Talking about feeling trapped, hopeless, or like a burden. Giving away possessions. Saying goodbye in a way that feels unusual. Or just seeming like something in them has changed.

The second thing I would tell people is not to be afraid to ask directly when they are worried about someone. You do not need perfect words. You do not need to become their therapist. You need to be calm, direct, and willing to help connect them to support. The worst thing we can do is let someone sit alone with the belief that nobody sees them and nobody will stay with them through the hard part.

The third thing is that awareness is not enough. We have had plenty of awareness. Some of it matters. A lot of it is noise. The real question is what happens when someone finally says they need help. That window can be short. Sometimes it is a few days. Sometimes it is that night. If someone asks for help and the answer is a waitlist, a voicemail, a bad referral, or an appointment a week away, then we should be honest about the gap. That person needs timely, competent, human support.

I helped start what became Forge Health's veteran and first responder work because I saw the gap up close. Too many veterans and first responders were being treated by systems that did not understand the culture they came from, the trauma they carried, or the way substance use and mental health often overlap.

For me, this was never theoretical. As a Navy officer, one of the most painful experiences of my military life was losing a sailor to suicide. That kind of loss stays with you. It changes how you see the problem. It makes the stakes very real.

I also understood how difficult it can be for veterans to find care that does not make them explain themselves before they can even begin to heal. A veteran should not have to teach a provider what military service does to a person. A firefighter, police officer, EMT, corrections officer, dispatcher, or nurse should not have to translate trauma to someone who has no frame of reference.

That is why culturally competent care matters. It is not a slogan. It can be the difference between someone staying in care, or walking away.

My mission is to reduce isolation, improve access to care, and make it easier for people to ask for help earlier, without shame, judgment, or delay.

That is also why NAVFRW (National Association of Veteran and First Responder Wellness) matters to me. NAVFRW exists to strengthen the network of organizations serving veterans and first responders, share what works, and help improve access to care. No single organization can solve this alone. Veterans, first responders, families, clinicians, nonprofits, government agencies, and community providers all must be part of the answer.

People do not need slogans. They need connection that is real. They need families and friends who know what to look for. They need leaders who take this seriously outside of awareness months and memorial posts. They need care that is available when they ask for it. And they need providers who understand the world they come from.

That is the work. Reduce isolation. Ask directly when you are worried. Move quickly when someone asks for help. Make it safer for people to say they are not okay. And stop pretending strength means suffering in silence.

Email: eric@dcstrategies.com

dcstrategies.com

navfrw.org

For anyone in immediate danger or crisis, call or text: 988

Veterans, service members, and their loved ones, call: 988 and press 1

Text: 838255

Email: www.VeteransCrisisLine.net

Crisis Text Line: Text HOME to 741741

Safe Call Now for first responders and public safety personnel: 206-459-3020

COPLINE for law enforcement officers and their families: 1-800-267-5463

SAMHSA National Helpline for mental health or substance use treatment referrals: 1-800-662-HELP, or 1-800-662-4357

NAMI: nami.org

National Association of Veteran and First Responder Wellness: navfrw.org

Allison L. Sharpe LCMHC, PLLC:

Allison L. Sharpe LCMHC, PLLC is a New Hampshire based psychotherapist with over two decades of experience. Sharpe approaches therapy as an interactive process and an eclectic clinical orientation with a focus on Cognitive Behavioral Therapy (CBT), Mindfulness, Internal Family Systems (IFS), and Interpersonal Therapy. Additionally, Sharpe specializes in suicide prevention, intervention, and postvention, and works with survivors of suicide loss. She has a pragmatic list of three main factors to watch for if someone you love is struggling.

One: Overt language is obvious: "I want to kill myself. I'm just going to do (X) to myself," or words of that nature. It's important to look for coded language like:

"I'm just tired," or "I just want to sleep."

"I can't keep doing this."

"I just want to be alone."

"I want to go home." (If not referring to a physical home).

"If anything happens to me, promise to take care of . . ."

"I'm just stressed out," or "I'm having a hard time."

"No one cares," or "They'd be better off without me."

"I'm a burden," or "I'm to blame."

"I just wanted to thank you for all you've done."

Two: In talking with a person who is suicidal, it can be helpful to approach the conversation in terms of Suicidal Intensity (vs Ideation): which is less pathologizing and more personal. It is a dynamic term that assists clinical conversations and helps with introspection.

Three: Language Matters: Died by suicide or took their own life. *Not* committed suicide. And in speaking of suicide death: either completed suicide (died by).

Allison L. Sharpe
(603) 236-7774
asharpetherapy@gmail.com
asharpetherapy.com

Amy M. Cook, BA MBA:

Amy M. Cook, BA MBA is the Director of Training for NAMI NH, and the National Trainer of CONNECT, Suicide Prevention & Postvention. She serves as Chair of the NH State Suicide Prevention Council, and has held positions as Director of the Division of Community Based Military Programs at NH Department of Military Affairs and Veterans Services, been part of the NH Military Leadership Team, and the Governor's Challenge to Prevent Suicide Service Members Veterans and their families. Cook has been a Representative to the US War College National Security Seminar Leadership, with the mission statement: To build communities of readiness where individuals are prepared to recognize distress, engage in direct and compassionate conversations about suicide, respond effectively in times of crisis, and support healing in the aftermath. Preventions include what happens before and after loss.

Cook's recommended resources:

988 Suicide and Crisis Lifeline: Call, text, and chat with trained counselors 24/7/365 across USA and territories.

Veterans Crisis Line: 988 and press option #1 or text 838255.

NH Rapid Response: 833-710-6477. Trained counselors can deploy mobile crisis response teams to communities as needed.

211 NH: Provides access to The Doorway, NH's network of substance use disorder access points. Call 211 or go to 211nh.org. Identify yourself as a veteran to access specific veteran military resources.

Cook's best practices for supporting suicide prevention among veterans, servicemembers and their families:

One: Recognize changes, not just risk factors. Pay attention to changes in behavior, mood and/or routine, especially when they are sudden, significant, or out of character. These changes may be subtle especially with those in the military or first responders who are otherwise focused on strength and self-reliance.

Two: Strengthen connection and belonging, which are powerful facets and particularly important among veterans, servicemembers and their families. Reinforce peer support, unit cohesion, family relationships and community ties. Create environments that are safe to talk about stress, transition, loss, and identity.

Three: Be prepared to respond before a crisis happens. Suicide is not just about awareness; it's about readiness. Be willing to set aside your own discomfort to ask directly about suicide. Listen without judgements, respond calmly, and help to connect the person with additional support as needed.

Four: Provide help after suicide loss. Those who are impacted by a suicide loss are at greater risk themselves. Acknowledge the loss, reduce isolation and support people in grief.

Jeff Ladieu, Executive Director of Camp Resilience:

Jeff Ladieu is the Executive Director of Camp Resilience in New Hampshire's Lakes Region. It provides an outdoor experiential opportunity for members of the military and law enforcement, and their families, to support their mental, emotional, spiritual, and physical wellbeing. Ladieu knows the pressure of military and law enforcement roles, having served himself for over two decades, including in the 75th Ranger Regiment under US Army Special Operations Command, as NHSP Captain, and in NHSP SWAT under Chris AuCoin.

In his own words, Jeff shares this message: I was proud to serve beside Chris for many years with the New Hampshire State Police. We were both veterans, teammates, and brothers in the job. Chris was my SWAT Commander, but more importantly he was the kind of man you could always count on… loyal, tough, humble, and always there for others. He led from the front in the Marines, in law enforcement, and in life. He will forever be missed.

One thing Chris's life reminds me of is that even the strongest people can carry struggles we may never see. We need to check on each other more, especially the ones who always seem "fine." Stay connected, have the hard conversations, and never view asking for help as weakness. In our professions, we're trained to protect others, we also need to protect one another.

If sharing Chris's story helps someone reach out, check on a friend, or ask for help, then his legacy continues.

988 Suicide & Crisis Lifeline — Call or text 988

Veterans Crisis Line — 988, Press 1

Safe Call Now — Confidential support for first responders and veterans.

If you are in crisis, please call the National Suicide Line by dialing: 988, then press 1

Copline: 1-800-COPLINE (1-800-267-5463): This resource is a confidential, 24-hour law enforcement officer hotline manned by retired law enforcement officers trained in active listening.

DoD Safe Helpline - Hotline for members of the DoD community affected by sexual assault. A completely anonymous, confidential, 24/7, specialized service—providing help and information anytime, anywhere. Hotline: 877-995-5247

If you or someone you care about is having a mental health or substance use emergency, you can contact (call or text) 24 hours a day, 7 days a week.

Call/text 1-833-710-6477(NHRR)

Nationwide Resources:

VA.gov Home | Veterans Affairs

https://firstrespondercenter.org/ - Offers training for the First Responder community, as well as mental health resources.

https://responderstrong.org/ - Offers training for the First Responder community, as well as mental health resources.

Camp Resilience: https://www.camp-resilience.org/about

Retreat Partner Resources:

Clear Path for Veterans New England - to build a safe, supportive and respectful place for Veterans to seek the help and resources they need to successfully integrate into their communities. The family is an integral part of this and the first line of defense in upholding wellness.

Home Base - To heal the invisible wounds for Veterans, Service Members, and their families through world-class clinical care, wellness, education, and research.

Project Healing Waters Fly Fishing - dedicated to the physical and emotional rehabilitation of disabled active military service personnel and disabled veterans through fly fishing and associated activities including education and outings.

Veteran & First Responder Healthcare - provides dual treatment for service-members, veterans, first responders and their families, suffering from substance use and behavioral health disorders.

Wounded Warrior Project - Wounded Warrior Project is a charity and veterans service organization that offers a variety of programs, services and events for wounded veterans of military actions following September 11, 2001.

Northeast Passage | University of New Hampshire - Recreation Therapy and resources for leisure

HarborCare - Harbor Care - Housing, Healthcare, Veteran Services - New Hampshire - Harborcare provides housing, healthcare, and veteran services. There are Harborcare facilities across the United States.

Easterseals - Easterseals Disability & Community Services

Badger Wilderness Guide - https://www.badgerbasecamp.com/

Health & Housing:

National Alliance on Mental Illness New Hampshire (NAMI NH)

Lakes Region Mental Health Center

Liberty House

National Alliance on Mental Illness

American Foundation for Suicide Prevention

Give An Hour - Free counseling for current or past military members and their families.

Additional Websites and Informational Organizations:

American Foundation for Suicide Prevention: https://AFSP.org

New England Contact: Executive Director, Shamera Simpson, of the American Foundation for Suicide Prevention, Maine and New Hampshire Chapters: ssimpson@afsp.org (603) 318-8302

NH Suicide Prevention Council: https://preventsuicidenh.org

National Alliance on Mental Health (NH): https://www.naminh.org

Substance Abuse and Mental Health Services Administration (SAMHSA): https://www.samhsa.gov

Veterans Crisis Line: https://www.veteranscrisisline.net

Center for Workplace Mental Health: https://www.workplacementalhealth.org

American Association of Suicidology: https://suicidology.org

Sheena Bice, DMSc, LCMHC, MLADC, CCTP:

Sheena Bice, DMSc, LCMHC, MLADC, CCTP, is the Head of Veteran and First Responder Services, Forge Health VFR Founder, Shield and Compass Counseling and Consulting. Here, she presents the Rule of Three in Suicide Awareness, Education, and Prevention.

One: Look beyond the obvious warning signs. For veterans and first responders, suicide risk may not always present as sadness or direct statements of intent. It may show up as withdrawal, irritability, increased substance use, reckless behavior, sleep disruption, loss of purpose, shame, anger, or statements that sound like burden, defeat, or "being done."

Two: Pay attention to transitions and identity loss. Risk often increases when someone is disconnected from their role, team, mission, department, unit, or sense of usefulness. Retirement, injury, discipline, medical leave, divorce, loss of access to weapons or duty status, and separation from service can all carry clinical significance.

Three: Prevention is not only a crisis response. Suicide prevention starts long before someone is actively suicidal. It includes building trust, reducing stigma, improving access to culturally competent care, strengthening peer connection, addressing substance use and trauma, and making help-seeking feel operationally acceptable rather than personally weak.

Forge VFR Mission Statement on Suicide Prevention:

At Forge VFR, we believe suicide prevention for veterans and first responders must be proactive, culturally informed, and rooted in trust.

These populations are often trained to function under pressure, minimize distress, and keep moving despite pain. Effective prevention requires more than a hotline number. It requires systems that recognize occupational trauma, moral injury, cumulative stress, identity disruption, and the real barriers that keep people from asking for help.

Our mission is to create pathways to care that are accessible, clinically sound, and grounded in respect for service, sacrifice, and lived experience. We aim to help veterans and first responders stay connected to purpose, family, community, and themselves before crisis becomes the only point of entry.

Additional Resources:

For immediate crisis support: Call or text 988, or chat through the 988 Suicide & Crisis Lifeline, or visit their website at 988lifeline.org.

For veterans, service members, and their loved ones: Call 988, then Press 1, text 838255, chat through the Veterans Crisis Line, or visit their website at veteranscrisisline.net. This support is confidential, available 24/7, and does not require VA enrollment. (Veterans Crisis Line)

SAMHSA 988 Partner Toolkit: samhsa.gov/mental-health/988/partner-toolkit

Forge Health: forgehealth.com

Anne T. Perriello, LCSW:

Anne T. Perriello, LCSW is the Chief of Police in Pelham, New Hampshire, with 25 years of experience on the job. She is also a Licensed Certified Social Worker. In her own words, Chief Perriello offers extensive advice, suggestions, and insight into noticing developing symptoms in yourself, colleagues, and loved ones:

Learn early on in your career, or your loved one's career, that your mind will attempt to drive your thoughts, emotions, and response to stress and trauma-related calls for service. You will need to exercise control over your thoughts and remain present in the moment. This takes practice and repetition. This profession exposes you.

PHOTO GALLERY

Brent and Paula, 1970

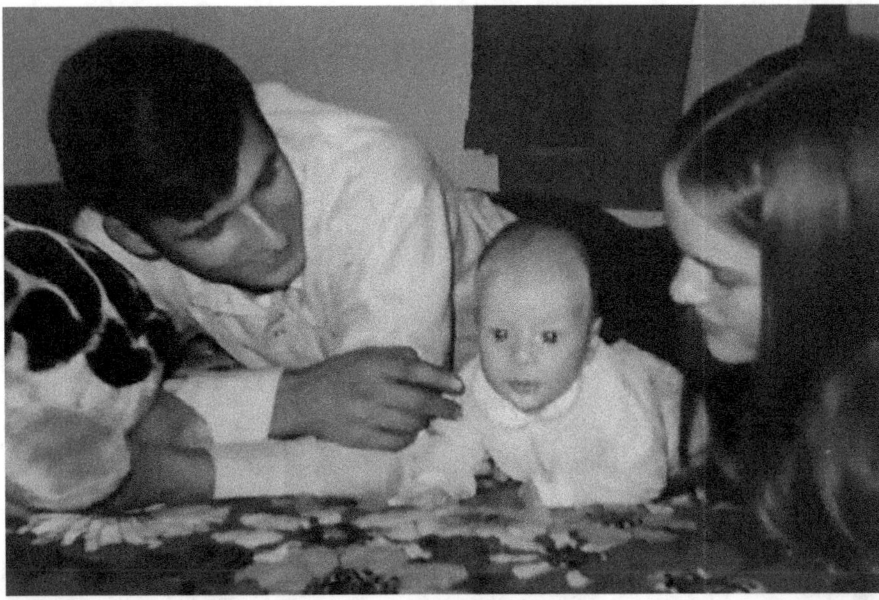

Brent, Paula, and Chris 1970

Chris and Fern, Memorial Day Parade, Jaffrey, NH

Chris on his dirtbike, Jaffrey, NH 1982

Brent, Paula, Nate, Chad and Chris, 1989

Chris pre-deployment, Camp LeJeune December, 1990

Chris and Kevin Sullivan, Kuwait 1991

Chris, Kuwait 1991

Chris, on duty 1991

Chris and troops, Kuwait 1991

Chris, Kuwait, captured enemy tank. 1991

Weapons Platoon, Kuwait, 1991

Chris and Tracy

NH Police Academy, Chris 1st upper left, Kevin Duffy bottom 2nd from left 1997

Chris, Kelsey, Bethany

Nate's Wedding, Chad, Nate, Paula, Brent, Chris

Chris, Tracy, Kelsey, Bethany, Lindsay

NHSP SWAT Coast Guard Station, Newcastle, NH 2008

Chris and Lindsay

Chris and Kelsey 2001

Chris and Bethany

Chris, Brent, Paula, March 3, 2022. Vero Beach, Florida

SWAT comp, Sean Haggerty, Chris 2006

NHSP SWAT COMP 2006

Chris training one of his German Shepherds

Chris and Chris Vetter

NHSP Major Chris AuCoin

Chris, NHSP press conference

Chris, NHSP press conference

Chris, Bethany, Lindsay

Chris with Lindsay - Hike

Hiking, Chad, Brent, Chris Nov 2, 2022

Brent, Paula, Bethany, Chris. March, 2022 Vero Beach, Florida

Chris and Brent. Mason, NH October, 22, 2022

Chris and NHSP Media Event

Chris atop Mt. Washington 2022

2019 accident en route to AuCoin home

Chris, cold weather training hike. Dec. 20, 2021

Chris, cold weather training hike

Chris, Phil Smith, wife Rachelle. Boston Marathon 2021

1st Battalion, 25th Marines Reunion. Buddy Hackett (2nd on left, Kevin Sullivan, 3rd on left)

Chris AuCoin, Boscawen Veterans Cemetery

www.ingramcontent.com/pod-product-compliance
Lightning Source LLC
LaVergne TN
LVHW052038200926
848481LV00005B/1720